Make Everyday Your Someday
The Guide to Living With Passion and Purpose

BY SUSAN MAREK

*Inside illustrations by*
Aislinn Marek, Emma Marek, *and* Abigail Shoesmith

*Book design & cover illustration by Russell Shaddox*

Copyright © 2016 by Susan Marek

All rights reserved. No part of this publication may be reproduced, distributed, or transmitted in any form or by any means, including photocopying, recording, or other electronic or mechanical methods, without the prior written permission of the author, except in the case of brief quotations embodied in critical reviews and certain other noncommercial uses permitted by copyright law.

Make Everyday Your Someday
The Guide to Living With Passion and Purpose

Written by Susan Marek

E.P.I.C. Publishing Services, LLC
www.epicpublish.com

First edition
ISBN 978-0-9913270-5-8

For more information or to order this title:
www.susanmarek.com

*To and For Jeff: We are in this together.*

## Acknowledgements

It takes a village to birth a book. In my village, there is much love and support, for which I am eternally thankful. I am grateful first to my husband, to whom this book is dedicated and written for. We continue to turn many of our Somedays into Everydays together. I am thankful also to my children, who are my Ego's excuse and my soul's mission.

Wendy Vincent, editor, publisher extraordinaire and fabulous friend: I am thankful for your wisdom, love and mastery of writing.

Beth Tiger, Mary Parent, Theresa Byrne and Eden Marie James — my Forever Four: Thank you for your love and support.

And to The Universe: Thank you for the magic and miracles.

# How to Use This Book ... or, Not

My Kindergarten teacher sent a note home with my report card, which stated something like: *"Susan needs to work on neatness and coloring inside the lines."* Yikes! I was five-that's a lot of pressure for a child who is just learning how to control their bodily functions, let alone master an awkward, waxy crayon!

This book is a fun mash-up of a scrapbook, coloring book, journal and shit-sorting tome. There are no rules with this book: as you read and progress through the exercises, you will figure out how YOU want this book to look and feel. There will be opportunities to doodle, color and paste your dreams onto these pages ... or, not. You can use a fancy fountain pen, marker or ballpoint to fill in the answers to questions; maybe a colored pencil is more your speed. Or, none of the above.

No one is watching or judging. This is YOUR personal retreat from your everyday life; it's a place where you are encouraged to dream, remember who you are and discover where you want to go. You make the rules on how you want to make this journey of self-exploration. Take it slow or speed through; draw your dreams or color the cartoons; print in pencil or compose in color. Or, all of the above. Make it your own!

The pages are purposefully printed on one side so you can journal, doodle, mind-map, list and scrapbook your way to making **Everyday your Someday.** As for coloring inside the lines, I leave that up to you. In my life, I have had minimal success at following those instructions. Metaphorically, coloring outside the lines leads to new ideas and makes something uniquely yours. It's similar to thinking outside the box or believing there is no box at all. This is your book, your journey, your life, your SOMEDAY.

**It's time to make EVERYDAY your SOMEDAY.**

# Table of Contents

Introduction . . . . . . . . . . . . . . . . . . . . . . . . . . . . . 7
1. Becoming Present . . . . . . . . . . . . . . . . . . . . . . . 31
2. Leggo, My Ego! . . . . . . . . . . . . . . . . . . . . . . . . . 51
3. Someday in Seven Words . . . . . . . . . . . . . . . . . 69
4. If/When/Then — The Power of Words. . . . . . . . . 87
5. Putting it all Together . . . . . . . . . . . . . . . . . . . . 97
6. The Game Plan . . . . . . . . . . . . . . . . . . . . . . . . 105
7. Divine Support . . . . . . . . . . . . . . . . . . . . . . . . 119
8. Dealing with Fear and Ego . . . . . . . . . . . . . . . . 129
9. Integrity . . . . . . . . . . . . . . . . . . . . . . . . . . . . . 141
10. The Domino Effect . . . . . . . . . . . . . . . . . . . . . 151
11. The Game Plan 2 . . . . . . . . . . . . . . . . . . . . . . 157
12. The Elevator Speech . . . . . . . . . . . . . . . . . . . 167
13. Practice Makes Practice . . . . . . . . . . . . . . . . . 175
14. Today is Your Someday . . . . . . . . . . . . . . . . . 187

Conclusion . . . . . . . . . . . . . . . . . . . . . . . . . . . . . 193
Resources . . . . . . . . . . . . . . . . . . . . . . . . . . . . . . 199
List of Exercises . . . . . . . . . . . . . . . . . . . . . . . . . 201
Write Your Day Away . . . . . . . . . . . . . . . . . . . . . 203
About the Author . . . . . . . . . . . . . . . . . . . . . . . . 223

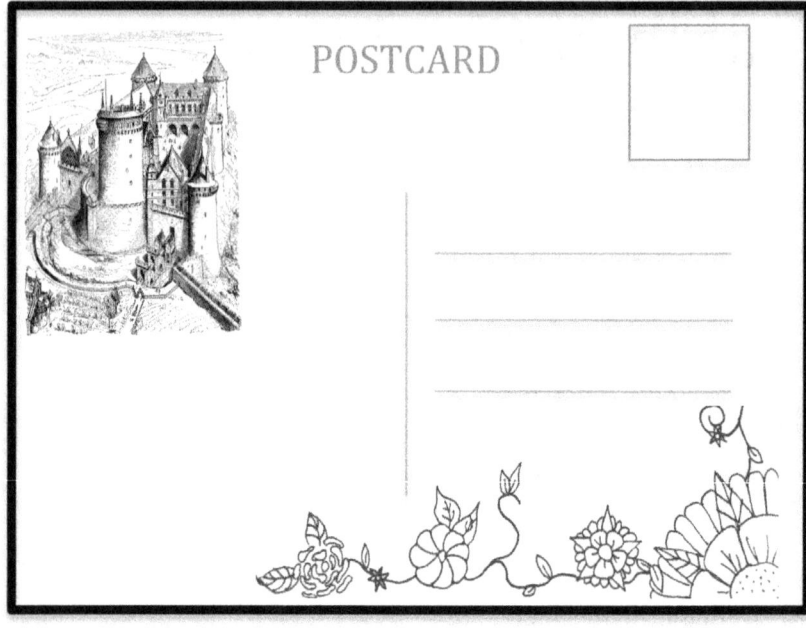

POSTCARD

# Introduction

The pitter-patter of the rain on the roof tiles entertained her on a lazy afternoon as she absentmindedly flipped through the glossy pages of the travel magazine on her lap. Page after page of palm trees, villas, beaches and skyscrapers in foreign, exotic places called to her gypsy soul.

"Someday," she whispered to herself, as she gingerly tore out a page about the castles of Scotland, taking care to not mar the colorful picture of an ancient stone fortress standing lonely and strong on an emerald green crag.

One longing sigh and pushpin later, the castle joined the other potential, albeit dusty, "Somedays" on the bulletin board. The top of a bougainvillea bush peeked out from behind the castle's keep, and the arm of a starfish extended out awkwardly from beyond the fortress' foundation. Layer upon layer of dreams waited patiently for her to say,

"It's time; my Someday is today."

As she turned away from the board, she tripped over the pile of laundry awaiting a good washing, one foot landing on her two year-old's muddy jeans and the other landing square on a Lego® brick. She collapsed on the floor, and holding her foot where there was still an impression of the wayward block, she began to bawl. Deep

# Notes

body-wracking cries came from her small frame as though her soul was crying out for something more. Her chest heaved as if it was trying to expel the years of neglect of her travel dreams.

A sort of mewing weaved its way in between the moans and weeping, faint at first, now growing louder and more desperate. She automatically held her breath to stop her own distressing sounds to focus on the new noise. *Sigh. The baby is up.* Wiping away the partially dried mud from her foot with an almost equally dirty t-shirt, she picked herself up off the floor and carefully sidestepped the scattered toys. Her eyes checked the clock.

"*The bus will be here soon and brother will be home,*" she said to the tow-headed baby now cradled in her arms.

She settled into the recliner and was preparing to nurse when she spied the bulletin board out of the corner of her eye. She heaved an audible sigh.

"*I hope they call today,*" she whispered. "*Maybe they will call. What if they don't? What if they* DO? *They probably chose someone else for that travel assignment.*"

Defeated, she kicked her foot off the floor, moving the chair enough to send the board out of her view. Staring at the small head now snuggled into her breast, she sighed and closed her eyes.

*Someday*, she promised herself. *Someday*.

"*Good book?*" The man's voice was an unwelcome guest in her literary daydream.

Her eyes stared up at him with a look of extreme annoyance and returned to their half-lidded reading position. She felt him back away from her cozy reading nook and disappear between the stacks. She settled back into

her word-induced trance only to be rudely pulled back into the real world by the buzz, buzz, buzz of her alarm. Angrily swiping at the screen of her phone, she frowned at how quickly her lunch hour had passed. Jamming her book into her overflowing tote, she made her way from her favorite chair, which was nestled in between biographies and mysteries, toward the front of the store, all the while running her index finger over the spines of the well-loved books neatly filed in the dark wooden cases.

As if emerging from a cave, she squinted and blinked hard when she stepped out into the noonday sun. The pungent smell of sauerkraut and well-cooked hot dogs assaulted her nostrils and she wrinkled her button nose in response. As she ambled down the sidewalk toward her office — well, really it was a drop of a cubical in a sea of gray metal-carpeted walls — she imagined she was walking down the boardwalk of a seaside village toward her very own bookshop. It was in her imaginary store that she fully came to life, her days full of assisting people in discovering a new country (or galaxy!) through the printed stories that overflowed from her shop. In her mind, she lounged behind a heavily distressed solid wood counter, thumbing through a new bestseller or an old classic that someone had brought in to trade. A tortoise-shell cat seeking her attention rubbed against her propped arm and the salty air of the sea blowing gently through the open door nourished her soul.

Again, her daydream was interrupted by another male voice asking *"Hey, lady. Which floor?!"*

"47," she mumbled, still half in her dream state as she reluctantly left the bright turquoise hues of her seaside shop to return her focus to the dull grey interior of the office building's claustrophobic elevator walls.

Sitting in her cube, she sadly turned to her computer

and logged in. The cursor blinked dully at her, awaiting her keystrokes. Sighing, she took one last glance at the book poking its corner out from the top of her tote and sighed.

Someday, she promised herself. Someday.

She gazed out the window at the greying marshmallow-like clouds that the plane appeared to be floating on.

"I wonder if they are getting rain down there?" she mused to herself.

"Mommy ... Mommy ... MOMMY!"

A sharp jab to her ribs by a very small finger brought her back to the reality of her life-one boy child, along with one aging cat tucked under a seat and all of their belongings packed into three overstuffed suitcases somewhere in the plane's crowded cargo area below them.

"I need to GO!" he shouted.

After three bathroom trips, two apple juices and a bag of pretzels, she and her boy buckled up for the final descent into Dallas. Even though it was just a short stop without even a plane change, she was still thrilled to be that much closer to their destination and that much farther away from their previous existence.

No more supervised visits with her counting the minutes until her boy was home. No more visits to the courthouse. He was hers — free and clear. And, she was out of there.

After the plane was cleared of Dallas-bound passengers, she and the boy walked up and down the aisles, stretching and yawning as the flight attendants cleaned and tidied the cabin for the next set of travelers. The flight deck door was open now, and the cockpit crew was

also enjoying a bit of freedom before the next leg of their flight.

"Hey there, son," drawled the captain. "Would you like to help me up here in the cockpit?"

The boy hesitated, but she pushed him forward toward the pilot.

"He would LOVE to! Thank you for inviting him up!"

She and the boy entered the small flight deck. The captain steered the boy into the co-pilot's seat and began showing him the mind-boggling number of switches and dials that took up every inch of space of the panels in front of them. She listened intently, mentally taking notes on each of the functions of the instruments.

"Here, son, you can put your hands on the steering wheel if you want."

"Don't be shy. It's ok." She grabbed her son's hesitant hands and gently placed them on the yoke. She held her son's hand tight on the rubber grips, her own fingers wrapped over his.

She moved her hands like she was steering and purred, "Now isn't that fun? Wouldn't it be fun to fly a plane?!!?"

Her son yawned and pulled his hand out from under hers and smiled a sleepy smile at the pilot. She grinned broadly at the man as her hands lingered a moment longer on the yoke.

As they exited the cockpit, the pilot handed the boy a pin, saying, "Here you go, son. You're a pilot now!" The little silver wings were almost as big as his hand.

"Umm, sir, may have another set of wings? For... my... nephew. We are going to be seeing him soon."

Eyeing her suspiciously, he handed her another silver pin.

"For your 'nephew'." He winked knowingly at her and turned to begin his flight preparations.

# Someday isn't a Day of the Week

With her son now asleep and another passenger clad in a dark pinstriped suit installed in the aisle seat next to them for the last leg of their journey, she gingerly fingered the plastic pin now safely stowed in her sweater pocket.

*Someday*, she promised herself. *Someday*.

Do any of these scenarios sound familiar? Perhaps your bulletin board is full of articles on technology, fashion clippings or even paint chips. You might hoard decorating magazines by the dozen; or, e-newsletters might crowd your inbox, all electronically brimming with the latest and greatest news on the theatre industry or travel destinations. Your hand might be reaching for a new recipe book in hopes of applying for a cooking show contest or you might be singing in the shower with hopes to finally pursue that music career you put off to study something more "sensible."

Whatever your passion, there are always "*Somedays*" that lie in wait, ready to pounce, or maybe trounce, on your dreams.

"But, wait! That doesn't make sense," you say. "Dreams and Somedays go together!"

Not true. *Somedays* sound so good at first. You make yourself deals that you will do *xyz* after such and such happens.

For example,
- *Someday*, you are going to travel the world when the kids are in college.
- *Someday*, you are going to start your own business after you have 10 years of experience under your belt.

- *Someday*, you are going to retire and move to *fill in your favorite exotic location here* after you have "done your time."
- *Someday*, you are going to go back to school for your degree so you can do the job you were born to do.
- *Someday*, you are going to finish and publish that novel you started back in high school.

All noble thoughts, to be sure, but I have to stop you right there. I hate to be the one to burst your bubble, but as your comrade-in-arms against waiting for *Somedays*, I must. I couldn't, in good conscience, let you continue thinking that any of your *Somedays* will actually arrive.

The truth is **Someday isn't coming.**

It isn't going to come after you win the lottery. It isn't going to come after the kids are that little bit older. It isn't going to come after you retire. *Someday* is not a day of the week or a holiday on the calendar. It isn't a specific year, day or month in your relatively short life span.

Rather, it is something we (isn't it nice how I am choosing to voluntarily take partial responsibility for such a horrible thing?) make up in order to make ourselves feel better. Feel better now? I doubt it. I have just taken away the one thing you have been clinging to, almost like a life raft, in order to make it through your day. Sadly, waiting for *Someday* to come has, in truth, crushed your dreams. It's time to bring those dreams back now. Breathe some life into those flattened, stale ideas. Manifest some miracles. No more excuses. Do you hear me? NO MORE EXCUSES.

**Let's make every single day your *Someday*.**

Merriam-Webster's Dictionary defines *Someday* as *"at some future time."* It's a vague and unremarkable definition and concept. Its partners in crime are: *eventually, finally, yet, sometime, sooner or later,* and *ultimately.*

When you use any one of these words, you are setting yourself up for disaster on the dream front. It's noncommittal, lame and downright detrimental to your life's passions. Your life's work isn't going to wait for *"sooner or later"* or *"eventually."* These words only postpone your true life for later. And, later doesn't cut it when we are talking about your life because "later" doesn't always come like you expect it to. Later is just an excuse we feed ourselves in order to cling to the possibility that we might actually do the things we say we are going to do "someday."

Making *Everyday* one of your *Somedays* might seem like a lofty goal, something unattainable. And, in your current frame of mind, it is. I mean, could you really drop everything and enroll in flight school right this very minute? My guess would be no. So, in order to bring back your dreams and really start living the life you have always wanted, we need to get grounded.

Before we move forward, let's back up for just a moment. *"Bring back your dreams and start living the life you have always wanted "*sounds extremely cliché, but it is what you want to do, isn't it?

Since you are reading this, you are probably thinking your dreams are gone; they went up in a cloud of smoke, never to be heard from again. But, I sense there is a glimmer of a small flame still burning. I know that a little part of you that hasn't given up hope yet is dying to be acknowledged and that's why you picked up this book.

**Good news! Your dreams aren't really gone!**

They are in hibernation, waiting for winter to turn to spring in order to allow your deepest dreams to grow into reality. The most ironic part? Your dreams are hiding *inside* your *Somedays*, waiting for you to wake up. Yep, that's right. They are within the very thing that is keeping you from them, right under your nose.

## Helpful hint reminder on how to use this book:

Throughout this book, you will discover exercises designed to help you work through the process I call "revealing and releasing." I have given you blank pages adjacent to each text page to begin a journal to document the incredible work you are about to do. Use these pages to work through the exercises in the book. This journal will be the "physical proof" of your journey. You will understand the importance of physical proof later on in this book. Writing the exercises from this book in a journal will not only be cathartic, but also encouraging and inspiring on your personal journey.

This book is designed to assist you in teasing out your true-life passions and will help you get rid of the *Someday* excuse. Each day should be a celebration of you and the very unique work that you are here to do. By removing the blocks to your success, you will have the information you need to make *Everyday* your *Someday*.

I will be here every step of the way to cheer you on, hold your hand, ask the hard questions and wait while you contemplate each move. I have been where you are. In fact, I still have *Somedays* that I tackle. It's an ongoing process that is both eye opening and freeing. And, you will move through it at your own pace, revealing old passions and peeling back blocks that will reveal even more fabulous things.

This process is like an onion. It has layers and it may make you cry as you work your way through it. But, the flavor it adds to your life is well worth a few tears. You will keep uncovering and peeling until the life you are meant to live is revealed to you.

It is my wish for you that, through this book, your *Somedays* become your todays and they expose to you the life you were born to live.

**EXERCISE:**
*Creating Your Journal*

There is no "right way" to journal. A journal is a very personal thing and you should create it in a way that supports the work you are doing. If it is unnatural to the way you think or function, you will not use it. Just as people learn in different ways, we also record our most sacred thoughts and emotions in different ways.

Basically, there are only three things, or steps, to keep in mind when preparing to journal:

- **Medium:** The first step in journaling is to find the right medium. This book can be used as a scrapbook, doodle pad, sketchbook, planner or all of the above. This is about you, not about what everyone else is doing or what *they* say you should be doing. *Who are "they" anyway?* Make it your own.
- **Instrument:** The second step is choosing your writing instrument. Will you be using a pen or pencil? Crayons? Markers maybe? A mixture of different writing tools? Again, this is for you, so choose what makes you happy.
- **Style:** The third step is choosing your writing style. One more time: this is for YOU. There is no right or wrong way to do this. Will you write in complete sentences? Will you doodle your answers? Will you make bulleted lists? Compose answers in iambic pentameter? Perhaps you like to express your thoughts through watercolor painted images. Maybe it will be a combination of all of the above. Have fun with it!

If journaling becomes a chore, or is done in a way that is uncomfortable to you, you simply won't want to do it. Just as there are different learning styles, there are different journaling styles. It is important for you to find the personal style that will work for you.

Studies suggest that people tend to learn something well when they have read, written and listened to a topic. Because the goal of this book is for you to reveal, release and learn what you need in order to make Everyday your *Someday*, we are going to work on all three.

Use this book as a journal to work through the exercises detailed in this book. Yes, there are exercises you are going to have to work through, but I promise you won't sweat too much-they are designed to help you reveal and explore your dreams in order to live your life with passion and purpose.

I hope that this book inspires you, and your dreams become so big, that you will fill up the blank pages in this book and be "forced" to start another journal to hold all of your passions and discover your purpose.

In order to really focus on your passions and explore your purpose, before you begin each exercise in this book, we are going to use the blank pages at the end of this book to *"write away your day."*

Because the exercises in this book require you to be present and you can't do that easily with

your mind full of to-dos, *writing away your day* will help you to clear out all of the chatter that your brain holds onto unless it has somewhere to go. You will be reminded of this in the first exercise, but do it each time you sit down to work on your journal. Begin each day with the date so you can keep track of what is on your mind before you begin the exercises. We'll get to this in just a moment.

Just to give you an idea of how I work, I love comp books or Moleskine® books with Flair® pens in multiple colors. I keep scraps of paper torn from magazines and newspapers, ideas on drawn on napkins, travel brochures of dream destinations and printouts from websites tacked up on a bulletin board or stuffed in a folder. With this book, I have created my dream journal: a place where I can keep all my papers, lists and doodles together in a coherent format, where I can still color and write with my pretty pens.

It's time to get started with the *"write away your day"* exercise. Find the section in the back of the book with blank pages and take a few minutes to personalize it. You could pretty it up with some doodles, paste in a favorite picture, add a sticker or two or just go minimalist and start writing. Take a few minutes now to "brain-dump" and write down some things that are on your mind before we begin the first chapter.

**Be flexible, be honest and have FUN!**

CHAPTER 1:

# Becoming Present

*The present moment, if you think about it, is the only time there is. No matter what time it is, it is always now.*

– Marianne Williamson

We are part of the "drive-thru generation." People want the instant gratification of having everything their way NOW. We are in such a hurry that we can't even be bothered to spell THRU correctly (which annoys me to no end, by the way!). I confess that I too have succumbed to this need of immediacy and self-indulgence. I don't watch live TV anymore. I want everything on demand and ready when I want it. I want it NOW, not tomorrow, not later, not yesterday, but NOW.

Yet, while I am getting those things now, I am not actually experiencing the now part of it. I am going through (not thru!) a drive-thru on my way to something "very important" because I "don't have time." I am multi-tasking and living moment to moment in the future. My to-do list is a mile long and I am looking past the now to the future while I check things off my seemingly endless list of things I must get done NOW. Sometimes, I forget to stop, take a deep breath and settle into the present moment.

**The truth of things is in the now.**

The gift of life is in the now. When we breathe in the present, we are conscious of where we are gifting our energy. When we give living in the moment our full attention, breakthroughs miraculously occur and magic happens.

# Bullshit to Get Done List

Like the mother with the insurmountable mountain of laundry, we trip ourselves up when we are not focused on the present moment. We are either looking into the future or lamenting about the past, both of which do not benefit us when we are working to focus on creating magic in our lives.

Our to-dos and lamentations of what has or hasn't happened are subconsciously (or, or not) set up by us to derail the process of living our passions. Our lists keep us thinking about the future and not focused on the task at hand.

Even if your task at hand is a to-do list, looking at that with the intention of being in the present changes how we view what we need to do. If I look at my list while focused on being present to what's around me with the energy and attitude I am bringing to that task, I undoubtedly prioritize those tasks differently and remove those that do not serve me.

For example, on my to-do list is a plethora of phone calls, research and proactive planning. My daughter's birthday is three months away. If I don't start planning now, I might not be able to find something that we would want for the party. That's what I tell myself anyway. True? Probably not, but it's that kind of proactive thought that derails my valid tasks that I need to accomplish. I put out fires that haven't started yet. I constantly find things to busy myself with in order to keep myself from doing what I need to do to accomplish my life's purpose. This is a common trick we play on ourselves. You will learn to deal with this in an upcoming exercise.

When I am focused on the present, crazy and made-up shit like a birthday party necessity that is three months away won't find its way on to your to do list of the present moment. Gifting our precious energy to the now is how

we become aware of what is really important and allows us to move seamlessly into making the magic happen around our dreams.

**EXERCISE:**
*Becoming Present — A Reminder
to Write Away Your Day*
I'm going to ask you now to stop and relax before we go on. You have some hard work ahead and you need to be in the right frame of mind to continue on. Don't be afraid of the hard work. It is only hard because you aren't used to following your passions. We have been programmed to think that we are undeserving of happiness or that you have to work yourself nearly to death before you are allowed to enjoy life. NOT TRUE! Also, NOT FUN!

Busyness seems to be a virtue, not an aspect of having a full, satisfying life. Many people attach value to being busy; as if the busier you are, the better you are. Add extra points if you are busy with things that you not only dislike, but are also for others. It's a form of martyrdom. You give up your life in order to make everyone else happy. You give up your happiness and your life purpose in order to fit into what other people say you need to do in order to be successful, happy, the perfect partner, etc.

In the movie, "The Devil Wears Prada," Andrea, our heroine, sells her writing soul for an assistant job to pay the rent and get experience in a field she knows nothing about in order to eventually make it as a journalist. A million girls would kill for her job, she was told. You'd be crazy to give that up, she heard. While at this job, she compromises her personal life, spends countless hours working on tasks not related to her passions and takes advice from co-workers in order to fit in and please her very demanding and successful boss.

In the end (spoiler alert!), she quits her job in a most spectacular way and reconnects with herself, but not before losing her boyfriend and some integrity in the process. She wasn't being true to herself or her mission in life. She was creating a life full of busy because she thought she had to. She didn't have to. You don't have to.

**It's time for you to put yourself first!**

To begin that process, we are going to put our busyness aside and focus on the present, a necessary skill for making Everyday your Someday!

Let's begin by getting comfortable and take the next few minutes to write down everything that is on your mind, either in the space below, on the facing page or in the back of this book. And, I mean EVERYTHING! Things like: *my stomach hurts. I have to put the laundry in. When was I supposed to pick up little Johnny from school? I am worried about my mom. The dog has diarrhea. What color should we paint the kitchen?* Every. Single. Thing. Go ahead. Get it all out. I'll be here when you are finished.

How did it feel to *write away the day*? Refreshing? Annoying? Uplifting? Daunting? All of the above? However it felt is just perfect. Don't judge it. Just do it. You are going to do this before you begin any exercise we work through on *Someday*. Don't let your feelings on this process stop you from moving on; just write those down too and keep reading.

**There is a method to this madness.**

You MUST BE PRESENT in order to think about your dreams and get serious about making Everyday your *Someday*. If you are not present, you are either worrying about the past or the future, neither of which you can do anything about. One you can't change and the other is going to happen whether you like it or not. Tomorrow is coming regardless of how much energy you expend in worrying about it. Instead of putting forth the negative energy of worrying about something that COULD happen, wouldn't you rather spend the energy on CREATING a future you WANT to live in? Makes sense, huh? Onward and upward!

In addition to writing away your day, there are a few other ways you can center yourself and focus on the now. You could take a walk and be present to every sensation around you. What do you hear or smell? How do your shoes feel on the road or path? Do they crunch on the small stones or are they cradled in soft grass? What color is the sky? Is it robin's egg blue or a murky greenish color? How does the air feel passing through your nose and into your lungs? Is it crisp and cold or warm and heavy?

You can become present by creating a daily ritual around centering yourself for the day. You may already be doing this through the careful preparation of your morning coffee (pouring a steaming cup, stirring in a bit of cream and sugar, savoring the first sip as you gaze out

over the zinnias growing in your garden) or by an early morning yoga class at the studio by the sea where the salty air sifts into your nose as you breathe in deeper in downward facing dog pose.

If you don't have a way to center yourself and prepare for the day, consider this your homework. Think about some ways that you could inject some centering and pampering into your day. Maybe it is turning off your cell phone for a half hour while you make breakfast in order to focus on being present to your morning meal. Perhaps you could take a book outdoors during lunch to enjoy the sunshine and explore a world miles away from your cubicle walls.

My morning ritual is hopping in the shower and using that time to speak with the Universe. Sometimes I cry and complain, but more often than not, I am reveling in gratitude for the abundance in my life. And sometimes, it's both. The water wakes me up and stimulates me energetically to ready myself for the day ahead. I come out feeling refreshed, awake and prepared for my day.

We all have our routines and rituals that are unique to us and whether we know it or not, can make or break our day. Sometimes, our routines can be a block for us. Think back to a time where you couldn't find your lucky pair of shoes or how you got upset because someone used the coffee mug you use EVERY. SINGLE. DAY. When those special things are out of place or missing, we become panicked. Now we are present, but not in the way we should be. Our routines shouldn't become routine and we need to be open to changes and surprises as this is going to be key later on in making Everyday our *Someday*.

**EXERCISE:**
*Making your Someday List*

This is the part that you get to let your imagination run wild. You are going to wake up those tired dreams and bring them out of hibernation. You are going to give yourself permission to remove all of your self-imposed restrictions and rules about how life is supposed to be… like when you turn a certain age or reach a certain level of job you should be doing (fill in the blank). Put all of that type of thinking aside for this exercise.

Let's create your SOMEDAY list. No holding back. Let yourself go!

An example of a SOMEDAY list might contain items like:

- Someday, I want to learn Gaelic if I go to Ireland.
- Someday, I am going to live debt-free, probably when I retire.
- Someday, I am going to practice yoga everyday if I learn how.
- Someday, I want to learn to ballroom dance when I finish my education.
- Someday, I will fly in a spaceship when I'm older.
- Someday, if I have enough money to travel, I will hike the Himalayas.
- Someday, I want to read *Gone with the Wind* if I have the time.
- Someday, I want to write a mystery novel if I can think of a good enough plot.
- Someday, I want to visit all 50 states if I buy an RV.
- Someday, I want to swim the English Channel when I am a good enough swimmer.
- Someday, I want to ride the Orient Express.
- Someday, if I have enough money, I want to visit the Galapagos Islands.

*Someday*

MAKE EVERYDAY

- Someday, when I quit my job, I want to own a bookstore.
- Someday, if I win the lottery, I will buy a beach house.
- Someday, when I'm not so busy, I will go back to school for an advanced degree.
- Someday, if I have some land, I will plant a garden.
- Someday, if I travel to an exotic new city, I will try a new type of cuisine.

As you can see from the sample list, there is everything from reading to space travel. So many possibilities and none of them are wrong or bad. They are a starting point for you to begin creating your life from your dreams and passions.

In the space below or on the facing page, write down all your *Somedays*. Even the ones from when you were a little child. Be warned of that part of you that is going to try to edit your list even before it reaches the paper, telling you a certain *Someday* is silly, impractical or extravagant. DO NOT LISTEN TO IT AND DO NOT EDIT! Just write it ALL down and tell that annoying nagging part of you that all is well and you promise to go back later to take out all the frivolous stuff. That should appease that voice for now. Funny how we have to "trick" ourselves to really get to the heart of what matters to us.

Ready ... Set ... GO!

*Someday*

MAKE EVERYDAY

How did you do? Are you coming up blank? Are you shocked and saddened that you only thought of a few, or maybe no Somedays? Don't panic! It's a common problem. Sadly, we give up our dreams in exchange for *perceived* comfort, safety and acceptance. In reality, that perception doesn't hold up to the life we could lead if we were really following our passions.

I often hear, *"But I don't know* WHERE *to find my Somedays!"* Your childhood dreams are one place to look, but your favorite things are another clue to your Somedays. What are your favorite movies, books, TV shows, plays and destinations? What toys did you enjoy most as a child? What were your favorite classes in school? What do you do when you have free time?

All these things give us clues to our true selves. For example, one of my favorite books is *"Eat, Pray, Love"* by Elizabeth Gilbert (Penguin, 2006). It's not because of the fabulous travel or romantic encounters. It is the author's spirit of adventure and her love of life, in addition to her bravery at leaving her old life behind in search of her true path that turns me on and makes me say, "YES! *That is me, hidden behind my what ifs and can'ts."*

So let's try this again. Write, draw, list, doodle and imagine your Somedays in the space below or on the facing page. No holding back. Just go for it!

It is my hope that you ran out of room this time or used a second page because your *Someday* list was truly overflowing with unanswered dreams and passions. If you didn't, that's okay too. You can add to that list anytime you want.

**Remember, there are no rules to uncovering your passions and purpose.**

So, keep dreaming and *"Someday-ing"* after you put this book down and come back to your list as often as you feel the need to. Your list is going to change in unknowing ways as you move through this book. You may even feel like starting a new list a little later. That's okay too.

Being present is indeed a present to yourself as you begin to discover what fuels your passions and encourages you to make Everyday your *Someday*. Your *Somedays* are your dreams in disguise and being present helps you to stay focused on what is important to you and vital to your mission here in this lifetime.

In the next chapter, we will delve into some of the things that will crop up when you begin to dare to live your dreams. Have no fear! We shall hold hands and walk through uncharted territories together!

CHAPTER 2:
# Leggo, My Ego!

*I fed my Ego, but not my soul.*

—Yakov Smirnoff

I touched on this a bit earlier, but now we really need to delve into the nitty-gritty of *Someday*. Think back to when you have used the word "*Someday*." *Someday*, I want to buy a sports car. *Someday*, I want to be rich. *Someday*, I want to go to Hawaii. *Someday*, I want to start my own business. *Someday*. *Someday*. *Someday*. Now I want you to say your *Somedays* out loud. Go ahead. No one is listening. Just say it like you mean it.

How did that sound to you? Did it sound hopeful? Did it sound promising? Did it sound pathetic? Whatever you think it sounded like is absolutely TRUE ... to you. YOU are judging it. They are just words. Sounds put together to bring your own thoughts to the surface.

And, here's another secret: you have already judged your desire by putting SOMEDAY in front of it. Yep. It's true. You have already decided even before the sounds came from your mouth that you weren't worthy of a particular dream. The word SOMEDAY is that powerful, that devastating to your dreams that you have signed your dream's death warrant by uttering that seemingly innocuous seven-letter word.

Remember that *Someday* means at "*some future time.*" We are not doing our dreams justice by neatly organizing

them and shelving them under "*some future time.*" Do you recall when you were little asking your parents for a treat or to go to the park? If they were busy, they probably told you, "*Later...*" Your dream of savoring a sweet chocolate chip cookie or playing on the swings was postponed until the dreaded "*later.*" When we say *Someday*, we are doing the same thing, just on a bigger scale.

**Your true dreams, desires and passions are clues to your life purpose.**

Postponing those dreams, desires and passions means you are postponing your mission in this life and thus postponing your own happiness. And, this will simply not do. You are meant to live a full, happy life.

**You DESERVE to live a full, happy life.**

Touch back on the definition of *Someday* and how its use demeans the value of your dream/desire. What is a dream/desire? Merriam Webster defines a dream as "*something that you have wanted very much to do, be, or have.*" Put those words together and we have "*something that you have wanted very much to do, be, or have at some future time.*" Does the definition of dream conflict with *Someday*? Or, does it merely offer an excuse as to why we can't attain our dreams TODAY?

*Someday* is a word that should be removed from your vocabulary ... pronto! There is no room for it in your world full of possibility. Practicing being present will help you to catch yourself when you fall into the *Someday* trap. Being conscious of your word choice, which we will discuss in a bit, will help you avoid this pitfall. Thankfully, there is only one small part of you that uses the word *Someday* with abandon: your Ego.

# Ego

Ever since you were born into a human body, you have been trying to navigate this dense world as best you could. It would be a cruel joke to dump us here without some means of guidance and coping mechanism, so we were equipped with some internal compasses as well as a homeostasis mechanism to prevent us from straying too far from center. That mechanism is called the Ego.

The Ego is a tricky bastard, to be sure. Useful when we first begin to figure out our place in the world as a youngster, the Ego develops quickly, helping us mind our "P's and Q's" so we won't stray too far from the safety of our flock. While this is a good thing when we are small, it swiftly becomes a huge pain in the ass when we are ready to set out on our own and leave our sheep friends in order to pursue our dreams.

When we set out on our own, defying our Ego's wishes, we also will have other people's Egos to contend with. Why? Because, misery loves company. If our own Ego can't control us, perhaps the collective sheeple Ego (sheep+people=sheeple) mind of our peers can.

Here's an example of sheeple mentality: When Apple® first came out with the iPhone® (and this is true for each subsequent model), the lines for this new product were so massive that police were needed for crowd control.

People were waiting in line for days ahead of time in order to be one of the first customers to buy the new technology. I admit, that like many others, I was excited about the phone and even waited in a few lines myself. Coming from a geek family, I was well versed in the technology and understood its features. I knew how it would make me more productive and I loved the sleek new look.

After standing in a few lines, I learned that the majority

of people were not buying it for its features. Most were in line because it was an Apple® product and if you have one, then you are cutting edge and cool. Slick advertising and hype, as well as their friends, co-workers and acquaintances convinced them of that. I saw several get in line just because it was a line outside of an Apple® store. They didn't even know what the line was for! They only found out after asking a few minutes into the line. They were just being part of the sheeple flock!

It must harken back to our tribal days when it was vital to be part of a small community. We did things to please each other and to maintain group happiness. Everyone wants to be liked and appreciated, but when it is at the expense of our soul, it is neither healthy nor wise.

Your Ego might be telling you to buy this or that, take that job because you have to pay the rent, don't move there because you won't be able to find a job, etc. Your Ego and the sheeple Ego may seem to be powerful at first, but with a little slight of hand, it can be distracted, leaving you to continue on your path to your dreams.

**We need to give the Ego its moment in the spotlight because it deserves kudos for getting us this far.**

When we are very young, the Ego makes sure, first and foremost, that we are safe. *"Are you sure that's a good idea?"* and *"What if this happens?* THEN, *what will you do?"* These are common thoughts that Ego plants in our heads to get us to think.

Because Ego is focused on keeping you, the human being, safe and productive within society, maintaining a behavioral homeostasis is imperative. Not too far to the right, not too far to the left. Maintain current course. NO deviation.

For example, if you are in a job that sucks your very soul from your body each and every day and you see no

end in sight to the misery, your Ego will try to "help" you keep "safe" by telling you to stay put! "Don't quit!," the Ego protests. You will be out of work and that will make you even more miserable than you already are, Ego argues. Even though you hate getting up in the morning every day, if you didn't have this job, you would be homeless and living in a van down by the river, Ego rationalizes. Your friends will abandon you; your family will disown you and society will laugh at you for being a failure. So stay in your job. After all, it isn't that bad, says Ego. You do get free coffee and pens. And don't forget, SOMEDAY when you win the lottery, you will get a lot of satisfaction telling your boss how terrible he/she is and then you will be able to travel the world, doing what you want to do.

A-HA! Now you see where SOMEDAY comes in. You're your Ego's bargaining chip. Just do this or that, THEN you will be rewarded when SOMEDAY comes around. Ego is so desperate to keep the status quo that it sells you false hope with SOMEDAY. Ego will always encourage you to take the path of least resistance, even if the path is sad or hurtful. It is easier to stay with what you know, even if what you know sucks, than it is to venture outside of your comfort zone to pursue your dreams.

I said EASIER, but not BEST. The Ego is invested in you maintaining the way things are and in surviving. It is not invested in you going above and beyond mere survival because there are too many variables. Too many variables lead to too many unknowns. And in Ego's world, too many unknowns are not acceptable.

The phone rang in short, measured bursts, first breaking her train of thought and then, freezing her in her tracks.

"This could be it!," Ego exclaimed. "Don't answer it!"

Her palms began to sweat from the anxiety of the unknown, but yet there was a slight tickle in her solar plexus, a little thrill that was causing her stomach to flip. What if it was the offer she had been waiting for? They said they would be in touch and now they were calling!

"*It's probably not they,*" whispered Ego. "*They would have called you first thing if they wanted you. Just listen to the message later. You don't want to ruin your day.*"

Clicking on the disk icon, she saved her work and glanced at the caller ID screen. Unknown number. Sigh…not helpful. She tried to go back to her writing, but was distracted by the argument going on inside her head.

"*Pick up the phone! What are you afraid of?!*"

"I'm afraid of being rejected!"

"*You don't even know who's calling!*"

"I know it is the magazine calling to say no."

"*You don't know any such thing! Take a chance. It's only a phone, for God's Sake!*"

The phone stopped ringing and rolled over to voicemail, which was muted to avoid distractions. I'll deal with it later, she thought.

# BAAAAAAAAAAAAAAA

We can't talk about our own Ego without also addressing the collective Ego of the sheeple mind. When we are born, we enter into the flock of sheeple, people who often follow each other blindly. We eat when everyone else eats. We baaaaaa when everyone else baaaaaas. We move because the person in front of us moves.

# Notes

For fun and to put the theory into practice, try this at a stoplight: carefully, SLOWLY inch up on the person in front of you, leaving enough room to safely maneuver if need be. Now look in your rear view mirror. Almost without fail, the person behind you will do the same. Why? Because you did it. Sheeple mentality.

Have you ever voted for someone or some ballot measure because a friend told you it was a good idea? Did you research it yourself? Did you educate yourself on the facts beforehand? Was it in your best interest or were you just going with the flock?

**The way we think about and interact with our flock influences our Ego.**

Remember, the goal of the Ego is to MAINTAIN and PRESERVE. In Ego's opinion, it is in our best interest to baaaaa right along with everyone else. This can lead to unhealthy compromises, lost dreams and missed opportunities. Ego's nod to the flock is not peer pressure; it is how it maintains your homeostasis by the choices you make within yourself without direct outside influences. It is done through observation of others and our innate desire to please and fit in. Yes, we are all people pleasers at some level. It is our human nature, proven time and time again through scientific research. Studies have been done on how when offered cash with the choice to share or not share with another without repercussions, people more often than not choose to share their bounty with a complete stranger. We are born with the desire to fit in and make friends. It's human nature at its very core.

So what about peer pressure? The flock is heading toward a cliff. They are all gung ho about going over the edge. It must be the right thing because everyone in front has already done it and they haven't come back complaining. It can't be a baaaaaaaad idea or someone would

have said something. Right? Just come along- if you don't like it, you can leave. We won't like you if you make a different choice. All the sheep are doing it.

Collective Ego destroys individual dreams if you choose to participate. Society says get a 9–5 job and provide for yourself and your family. Work until you are exhausted because anything less means you are lazy. We are swayed by polls, advertisements, movie stars, well-placed products in a blockbuster movie. Our Egos are continually bombarded with sheeple propaganda. Don't think for yourself. Let someone else do that work for you. The Collective wants a stable, reliable participant. No wild cards, please. That's way too risky.

Some of you might be thinking, "*How conspiracy theory-ish!*" I admit, it does have the bones of a good sci-fi movie. Perhaps that was a bit dramatic, but it got you to THINK, didn't it?!

**EXERCISE:**
*What is YOUR role in the flock?*
Turn this into a formal exercise. Just for one day, I want you to pay particular attention to the motivation around your choices. You are going to examine almost every choice you make.

For example, while in the shower, look at the products you are using. What was your motivation in purchasing them? Did you buy them based on ingredients, packaging, marketing or recommendation from a friend? Do the same with your food choices, clothing choices, etc.

Then, pay attention as you go through your day to your interactions with people. When you agree to meet someone for lunch, are you doing it because YOU want to or because you feel obligated to? When someone asks for your opinion on something, are you telling him or her

# The choices I made today

what he or she wants to hear or are you telling him or her what you really think (diplomatically, of course!)?

In the space below and on the facing page, record your findings. Were you making decisions based on your own desires? Or, were you going along with it to fit in? Were you captivated by slick marketing and persuasive talk? Or, did you decide based on your own research and needs? Did you CHOOSE to be where you were or were you going with the flow? Again, NO judgement. It's just what IS in this moment. It doesn't mean it will be this way in the future. We have the freedom to change our behavior, thoughts and decisions.

**We are in a constant state of awakening to our own power of choice and circumstance.**

Your heart knows what is best for you and acts like a compass to point you in the direction of your life's purpose. When you get wise to Ego's tricks and learn to distinguish Ego's voice from your true voice, magic happens. You begin to move forward toward your passions and start the process of making each day your *Someday*.

The beautiful thing is that you are awake now to your own power and can choose to go anywhere and do anything you like. No more individual or collective *Somedays* to hold you down. No more falling for the *Someday* trick of postponing your happiness.

**Your *Someday* begins now!**

CHAPTER 3:

# Someday in Seven Words

*Why say no when saying YES feels so good?!!?*
–Tim Tiger

Our world loves acronyms. We love to text them. We love to make them up. We love to use them in letters, at work and in everyday conversations.

| | | |
|---|---|---|
| SOS | ASAP | AWOL |
| KISS | TTYL | BFF |
| MIA | BTW | DOA |
| LOL | FYI | AKA |
| USA | WTF | MO |

Allow me to digress for a moment and indulge in the sheeple mentality of creating an acronym to simplify and hopefully enhance my point. Here is my acronym for SOMEDAY:

> **Some**
> **One**
> **Makes**
> **Excuses (and)**
> **Doesn't**
> **Answer**
> **YES!**

These seven little words cause big trouble. Someone (that's you) makes up… stuff. You convince yourself that you would be better off staying put instead of _____ (fill in the blank with your *Someday*).

We consciously choose to say NO instead of YES when Ego starts whispering things like *"that would be very irresponsible of you! What are you going to do when that fails? You are going to ruin your life!"*

**Where in your life are you not answering "YES!" to the questions your heart and soul are asking?**

Realize your Ego may pout a bit (or a lot!) when you do decide to say yes to your passions. Ego doesn't like to be told no, much like a two-year-old. And, it's OKAY for it to stomp off and sulk for a while. Don't worry, it will be back, probably with a fresh argument. What is important is that you say "YES!" and get on with making everyday your *Someday*!

Her son tucked snugly in bed, at last she had time to return some emails and do some research for her proposal at work. Settling into her chair, she sighed as she began pounding away at the keyboard, jumping from website to website in search of the needed data. Her fingers reached for her mouse and, instead, landed on the pilot's wings that she acquired on the flight to her sister's home, now her home, albeit temporarily.

She laughed to herself. The cheap silver paint was actually wearing away from all of the absent-minded rubbing she did to it when she was stressed. Next to the wings lay a pamphlet from the local flying school that her sister had brought home for her a few days ago. "Learn to fly!" it promised in large yellow letters that were hanging in the air above a picture of a giddy couple behind the controls of a small airplane.

> "Just go for the introductory lesson. I'll even pay for it," her sister proposed.
> "No. I can't. I couldn't ask you to do that and watch my kiddo. No, not now. Maybe in a few months when I have my own place."
> Someday that will be me, she told herself. *Just a few more months, then maybe I will try it.*

**EXERCISE:**
## NO

This is the part where you get to write down all the things to which you have said NO; NO WAY; No, thank you; Nuh-uh. We get to act like a two-year-old again. Their favorite word is "NO!" Two-year-olds are exploring their own sense of power and boundaries. (I have also discovered recently that it is also a teenager's favorite word.) Why does a two-year-old (and my teenagers) act this way? Again, it's all about power and boundaries.

Just write down in the space below and on the facing page all the things you have passed on. The "because" is the next part; this is just for the NO statements.

This is a judgment-free zone to write things like: *No, I can't go to that school; No, I can't apply for that job; No, I can't go on that fabulous trip to Europe; No, I can't major in that.*

YOUR SOMEDAY

**EXERCISE:**
*I CAN'T*

Are you surprised at all by your No list? Perhaps you are shocked at how many potentially awesome things you have turned away in exchange for what you thought was safety and security.

Now, we are going to work on the "because" part of the previous exercise. In the space on the facing page, write down all your reasons as to why you can't/didn't follow your heart's desires that you listed in the previous exercise. NO judgment or editing allowed. Just write. We will pick it apart later and give your Ego a little thrill.

Here's an example list.
- (No, I can't go to that school.) It's too far away/expensive.
- (No, I can't apply for that job.) I don't have enough experience.
- (No, I can't go on that fabulous trip to Europe.) I have small children and they will die if I leave for a week.
- (No, I can't major in that.) I won't be able to make a living with it.

**Why say NO when saying YES feels so good?!!?**

A dear friend of mine, Tim Tiger, has some wisdom that he loves to impart. With a twinkle in his eye and a smile on his lips, he says, *"Why say no when saying YES feels so good?!!?"*

YES, I will start my own business! YES, I will go on that fabulous trip to Europe! YES, I will take a ballroom dancing class!

I love that wise, wise man. Now, of course, the caveat here is that the YES is in sync with your soul's purpose and desires. Disaster strikes when we go rogue and start chaotically down a path of self-destruction, all the time

declaring it's our heart's desire and such.

Sneaky Ego! When you don't take the time to listen to your soul, you might, in a blink of an eye, have sold your home, depleted your 401k and are following your "heart" to Europe to paint along the Seine. Odds are that although painting could be one of your passions and part of your life's purpose, drastic and impulsive moves aren't. We will talk more later on how to avoid that pitfall and how we know it's our soul speaking and not our Ego.

Although I have been tempted a few times by the patisseries and fine wines of France, I haven't abandoned my family for what would surely turn out to be a disastrous European wild goose chase, looking for my heart's desires in the antique shops and cafés of Paris.

**Remember this: where you are in this very moment is exactly where you need to be to start this journey.**

Where your journey leads will be found here, working on making *Everyday* your *Someday*. When you begin picking and choosing your Somedays, you will be surprised at what stays and what goes. I want to share with you two of my *Somedays*.

*Someday*, I am going to visit American's largest mall and spend my day shopping. I hear there's an amusement park built inside. I can drop my kids off to ride roller coasters and I can sneak away for some retail therapy.

*Someday*, I am going to be fluent in French. I am going to be able to read, write and speak with proficiency so I can travel easily throughout France. I also will be able to read history books in French for my research.

Anyone coming with me to the mall? How about France?

Yes, I like to travel, but I bet even though I live in the US, I will get to France before I will get to the Mall of America. This is because there are two different types of

# Notes

*Somedays*. The first type is the **Trivial** *Someday*. These are the things we think would be fun or exciting, but are not essential to our life plan. I saw the Mall of America once on TV and thought it would be kind of neat to visit it once just to see what it is like. I am not going to go out of my way to go there. I wouldn't plan a vacation around shopping there. But, if I am ever in Bloomington, Minnesota, I will swing by and check it out.

The second type is the **Mission Imperative** *Someday*. These are the "to-do's" that must be done because they are essential to our life's purpose. These goals or "dreams" have been with you from before birth. They are agreements you made with the Universe long before you were dropped into that little human body. You have had an interest and/or passion for things related to your mission since you were little.

I am absolutely sure that the mall is not in my Universal plan, but writing and teaching are. Some of you might be thinking that learning French isn't **Mission Imperative** for me. How is that related to teaching? It's a cheap excuse to go to Europe and eat baguettes and pastries. I assure you that it is truly part of my life's work because it enables me to do the research I need to do to complete my writings. Learning French is a stepping-stone on my path. It is these stepping-stones that give me the tools I need to stay on my path.

But, now I've opened that can of worms about "God's Plan" and the like. Well, I'm just going to free those worms and recycle that can. Trust me when I say that you have a unique and divine purpose. Because you are still here and reading this, your mission isn't over yet.

On the journey to making every day your *Someday*, you just might find out a bit about what you are supposed to be doing on this Earth. I would say that's a nice perk of

# Notes

all the writing and thinking you've done so far in our time together. Aren't we here to figure out our purpose and follow that passion?

**EXERCISE:**
*Classifying your Somedays*

In this exercise, you are going to flip back to your original *Someday* list and next to each one, write a "T" for **Trivial** or an "MI" for **Mission Imperative**. If the idea of having to classify *Somedays* based on your life's purpose makes you break out into a cold sweat and gives you heart palpitations, have no fear. You are not alone. This exercise is not meant to cause panic. It is meant to help you narrow things down a bit so you can get down to the business of living a life full of purpose and passion.

Here is a quick test you can do with each *Someday* to help determine its importance in your life: Close your eyes and take a moment to breathe into the *Someday* in question. Imagine yourself doing or being your *Someday*. How do you feel? Happy? Excited? Bored? Thrilled? Afraid? Play in that *Someday* for a few moments. Now, take notice of what your body is doing. Are there butterflies in your stomach? Are you tense? Is your body physically open or closed up? Your life purpose, or **Mission Imperative** *Somedays* are the ones that give you a little thrill and hope for a better future. They are the ones that might make you feel a little scared and excited at the same time, like being on a roller coaster. If they are making you tense or bored, then they are not **Mission Imperative**. They could be the collective Ego's idea of your future or just a little distraction to steer you away from your passions.

# Regrets... I've had a few

Example:
T— *Drive down the entire West Coast of the US on Highway 101*
MI — *Learn French*
MI — *Teach a workshop on following your passions*
T — *Take a cruise to Alaska*

A note about this *Someday* list: This is a partial list of my *Somedays*. If I were a photographer, the "T's" might be "MI's" and vice-versa. Your classifications are yours and yours alone. Don't compare your dreams to other people's dreams. You are unique in the entire world and as such, turning your *Somedays* into *Everydays* will be a unique process, too. Now get classifying!

**EXERCISE:**
*I said, "No" when "YES" would have been so much better*

In this exercise, we are going to take that original list you just marked up and correlate it to the list you made a few pages back in the NO exercise. Using only the *Somedays* marked "MI", write down in the space below and on the facing page examples of when you said no to something around that *Someday* when yes would have felt so good. In parenthesis, write down what your Ego said to you about that. Be thorough. Be thoughtful. And, as always, NO judgment.

Example:
MI — *Someday I will learn to be fluent in French when I have time. I said no to majoring in French. (What are you going do with a French major anyway? You will only be able to teach. There isn't anything else a French major can do.)*

Before we move on, I want to say, "Great job!" The work you have just done will be some of the most challenging you do before this is over. So, pat yourself on the back and congratulate yourself on a job well done. It takes courage and some honest introspection to get this far.

As you move toward making *Everyday* your *Someday*, you will find that saying YES to opportunities and experiences that honor your soul's needs will become easier and less fear-filled. You will be able to move easily into a mental, emotional and spiritual space where your life's purpose, not Ego, is able to guide you in your everyday choices.

One of the most powerful tools you will have to assist you in making *Everyday* your *Someday*, is word choice, which will be discussed in the next chapter.

CHAPTER 4:
# If/When/Then— The Power of Words

*Words are singularly the most powerful force available to humanity. We can choose to use this force constructively with words of encouragement, or destructively using words of despair. Words have energy and power with the ability to help, to heal, to hinder, to hurt, to harm, to humiliate and to humble.*

–Yehuda Berg

Words are a collection of letters, which are symbols of sounds. The way we put those letters together is our outwardly way of expressing our thoughts and more importantly, intentions.

Words don't sprout from nothingness. Firstly, the ideas are formed within our head from our own thoughts and experiences of the world around us. We then arrange those ideas into cohesive thoughts that we then may or may not form into the spoken or written word.

The words you are reading were first born from my soul and brain, then nurtured and coerced into a logical form for you to read, ponder and assimilate. The words I choose to use make all the difference in the world in what I choose to do with them and how I process them. It is the same for you and for anyone who has ever written or spoken.

**Thoughts, then words, become your world.**

As John Greenleaf Whittier said, *"Of all sad words of tongue or pen, the saddest are these, 'It might have been'."*

I would like to add the word *"Someday"* to Mr. Whittier's list of sad words. Whether we say it out loud or just think it to ourselves, *Someday* has the power to destroy our passions. As I mentioned in Chapter 2, *Someday* is the Ego's bargaining chip, convincing you to maintain the status quo by promising you will get your opportunity later.

Unfortunately, when we begin looking back at the opportunities we passed up, we find ourselves wondering what might have been if we hadn't waited for *Someday* and had just said YES and followed our hearts.

Words become things in our lives. Things that change our paths, things that affect others. A YES from our soul can open doors to possibilities we haven't imagined. A NO from fear and Ego can block the way toward our happiness. Our word choices can change attitudes and subsequently, our lives.

**EXERCISE:**
*Say it like you mean it*

Try this on. Say each of the following out loud: I hate my job. I dislike my job. My job is okay. I like my job. I love my job.

Now, go back and say them out loud again, but this time pay attention to HOW you say it and HOW it makes you feel. Take your time with this.

Did you notice a difference in each phrase as you said it? I can hear you saying each one carefully, yet your tone changes with each new declaration. By the time you got to "I love my job," you could hear the exclamation at the end, couldn't you?

There is a world of difference of intention and energy behind the words *"hate, dislike, okay, like, and love."* Your word choice is extremely important because it is with your words that you are birthing your ideas and intentions and thus, your future. You thoughts, which are your soul's ponderings and desires, are brought to life in this world through the written and spoken word. From these words will come action, which will help to manifest those *Somedays* into reality.

If not then, then when?

Our choice of words helps to create our future. In the idea of *Somedays*, there are two words that can make a huge difference in how a *Someday* manifests.

*IF I win the lottery, I will quit my job and move to the beach.* Yes, please! I would like that a lot. Sandy beaches for miles and warm weather to sooth my soul. But, I have made my happiness dependent on being a lucky gambler. Let's try this again.

WHEN *my kids are older, I will take some 'me time' and do some traveling.* Yes to this one as well! I am sure every parent has thought about this while changing his or her millionth poopy diaper.

Notice that the WHEN has changed things up a bit. Now I am not relying on luck to provide my fabulous future. I have inserted a bit of hope here by using WHEN. I have actually allowed myself to think that I will be able to have this reward at a future time determined by the growth of my children. Better odds than winning the lottery!

So, going back to the idea that words intrinsically matter, the difference between IF and WHEN is night and day. WHEN provides us with hope, which is the first step in allowing your soul's voice to speak.

**EXERCISE:**
*Turning IFs into WHENs*

Go back to your *Someday* list and re-write your **Mission Imperative** (MI) *Somedays* as WHEN statements if they are not already in that form. Use the space on the facing page, if you would like.

Take your time with this and notice where your Ego is trying to "BUT" in. "BUT, *you can't do that when that happens. It's too risky!*" "BUT, *you can't do that when you save that money. You need that for your retirement...*"

The BUT list can go on forever. **Don't listen to it now.** Put those WHEN's in there and let's keep moving. And, let's drop the *Someday* from it as well because these are soon to be your *Everydays* and todays.

Example:

*Someday, I am going to practice yoga everyday if I learn how.*
This becomes: *I am going to practice yoga everyday* WHEN *I learn how.*

*Someday, I want to visit all 50 states if I buy an* RV.
This becomes: *I want to visit all 50 states* WHEN *I buy an* RV.

*Someday, if I have enough money, I want to visit the Galapagos Islands.*
This becomes: WHEN *I have enough money, I want to visit the Galapagos Islands.*

Just a few tweaks with the wording and look how much the intention and energy behind the statement has changed!

Read your list out loud. First, the old statement. Then, the revised statement. Do you hear how powerful your

words are now? There is such a difference when you remove the *Someday* and the "iffyness" of your intentions.

Look how quickly you are moving forward on your commitment to changing your life through making these former *Somedays* your Everydays! Now, we are going to focus on putting it all together.

CHAPTER 5:

# Putting it all Together

*Choice is more than picking 'x' over 'y.' It is a responsibility to separate the meaningful and the uplifting from the Trivial and the disheartening. It is the only tool we have that enables us to go from who we are today to who we want to be tomorrow.*

–Sheena Iyengar

Your *Someday* list is a bit smaller now than when we started. We have driven out the **trivial** items, noticed where our **Ego** has prevented us from moving forward, become cognizant of our **word choices** and reworded our *Somedays* to fit a more hopeful model.

**You are now ready to make one of your *Somedays* a reality.**

Choose ONE *Someday* from your MI list and we are going to focus on that one from here on out. This doesn't mean we are abandoning the rest of them forever. We are just choosing one to take point in this mission to make *Everyday* your *Someday*. The one you choose will be the one to start the ball rolling.

I know you are anxious to begin living your life with passion and purpose. I also know asking you to choose between your **Mission Imperative** items is akin to asking

you who your favorite child is or saying you can't have both cookie dough ice cream and butter pecan. It's hard. As Sheena Iyengar in the quote above states, *"It (choice) is the only tool we have that enables us to go from who we are today to who we want to be tomorrow."*

So, I am asking you to choose only one to begin the process. If you were to choose to tackle more than one *Someday*, you would find yourself overwhelmed in no time. Taking on too much at once gives your Ego a foothold in the chaos and it begins to undermine your good intentions and progress. It then becomes super easy to make excuses about how you have no time to take the steps to realize your dreams because you are trying to do them all at once!

Taking on one *Someday* at a time allows us to ease into the process. It would be like trying to lift a 100lb. weight the first time at the gym. You need to exercise your manifestation muscles a bit and give your heart the chance to lead the way instead of the Ego.

Taking it step-by-step allows you to "prove" your intent to yourself and gives yourself time to adjust to your new way of thinking. And, don't forget the domino effect! Once you get going, the Universe conspires to help you reach your goals when you are following the path to your purpose. Things will seemingly happen as if by magic and soon you will be on to your second, third and fourth *Somedays*!

**EXERCISE:**
*The Chosen One*

Hopefully, you have been doing the "*Writing Your Day Away*" exercise as you have been going along to clear the brain chatter. If not, this is an excellent time to start (*hint, hint*). I want you to write down everything on your mind

right now. Unload your frustrations and concerns and capture them on paper, either below or in the dedicated space at the back of this book.

Get it all out so you are ready to work with your Ego in check and your soul ready to dance. GO!

Now, choose ONE *Someday* from your **Mission Imperative** list. The one that, in this moment, makes your heart sing and you giggle like a little girl in anticipation of its arrival into your life. Seriously, which one would bring you the most joy if it appeared before you right now? That's the one crying to be heard in this moment. Write it below or on the facing page.

Now, time to make just a slight adjustment to the wording. You want to reword your *Someday* declaration so that it is easy to remember and leaves no doubt as to your intent. As you learned in a previous chapter, your words

MAKE EVERYDAY

have power. So, use your power for good! Come up with one word or short phrase that represents your *Someday*. For example, "*When my kids are older, I will travel the world*" becomes TRAVEL THE WORLD.

**There is no more when. The time is now.**

Take your word or phrase and write it down on a card, piece of paper or sticky note. Place it somewhere that you will see it frequently — the bathroom mirror, the refrigerator or your nightstand are all great places. Decorate the card if you would like. Use bright colors, add stickers or even paint it. It is your reminder of fabulous things to come.

Now, take that word or phrase and write it on the facing page. Make it pretty, write it 1000 times, add your own pictures around that declaration to show yourself that you mean business. This is what you are going to dedicate many of your precious days of life to. Make it sparkle!

Because this is a new experience for you, it is to be expected that you will slip back into old habits at first. You need time to adjust to new thought patterns, new ways of speaking and new ways of looking at old relationships, situations and experiences. This card is your reminder that you have chosen to listen to your heart, not your Ego. You have taken the first step toward making your *Someday* a reality.

But, a card or a journal page is not enough to make it happen. We also need a game plan.

CHAPTER 6:
# The Game Plan

*Planning is bringing the future into the present so that you can do something about it now.*

–Alan Lakein

Before you begin to formulate your game plan, I want you to take a moment to congratulate yourself again for your incredible progress. I wasn't kidding when I said you were brave. It is hard work to take on your Ego and even the collective sheeple Ego. The work isn't over yet, but the rewards will begin to be realized as soon as the game plan begins to take shape.

Your personal game plan will not look like anyone else's. DO NOT compare your goal or progress with anyone. We are each uniquely gifted with exactly what we need to accomplish our mission. Thus, we cannot think that what another person has would be perfect for us. Just keep looking forward and trust that what you will need for the journey will be provided.

Take another deep breath before we dive into creating your unique plan. It's kind of like pearl diving. You take a deep breath and dive down into the water, swimming deeper and deeper until you find this little nugget of a shell. Then after dislodging it, you and this rough shell surface and when the oyster is popped open, a beautiful pearl emerges.

We are going to dive into creating this plan for your chosen *Someday* and will pop up from the depths with

some lovely personalized pearls of wisdom for you to follow on your road to success.

The game plan will have specific steps that you will take in order to make your *Someday* a reality. The steps are influenced by a few universal conditions that will help you with this process, like *movement*.

## Movement

Have you even seen (or smelled!) the difference between a stagnant pond and flowing water? The still water, although fresh and clear to start, turns dark over time, odiferous and toxic when not stirred and refreshed. The good organisms can die off, leaving only nasty bacteria and other unsavory organisms to populate the environment. Oxygen is almost nonexistent. Life cannot thrive under those circumstances.

Flowing water, on the other hand, is teaming with life and the conditions are supporting and nurturing. Organisms not only survive, but also thrive. Oxygen is plentiful and the current refreshes nutrients, removes wastes and prevents toxic build up.

Is your life stagnant and toxic? Are you gasping for oxygen or are you going with the flow? One of the big parts of the game plan is to take active steps toward your goal. These steps can be the tiniest of the tiny or a huge leap into the unknown. But, they are MOVEMENT, which is key to making *Everyday* your *Someday*.

FACT: **Stagnant lives go nowhere.**

It's that simple. Your days turn into weeks, your weeks turn into months, and before you know it, years have passed and you are no closer to really living your life than you were 1 year ago or even 10 years ago. It's sad how our dreams (which are usually your mission in disguise) languish in the stagnant ponds of our lives.

Well, that was quite depressing. Take a cleansing breath and let's take a moment to regroup and move forward a bit.

**EXERCISE:**
*Attitude of Gratitude? Really? For this?*

It is hard to be grateful for the muck and mire we are stuck in because, well, it's muck and mire. You know what it is, the undesirable and stagnant junk in our lives that we wallow around in hoping for a better future.

Right now, we are going to do something crazy. We are going to THANK it for being part of our lives. Yep. A HUGE THANK YOU to all the shit we have gone through to get to where we are.

**You would not be the fabulous person you are today without each and every experience, good and bad.**

Even the muck has given you its own gift of experience that has been integrated into you to make you spectacularly unique. So, time to write the thank you notes. Start first with the crap you are ready to release.

For example, a note I might write would say,

> *Dear Woman Who Tried Her Hardest to Make Me Feel Insecure,*
>
> *Thank you for your hurtful words. It gave me the opportunity to really evaluate who I am and not who others want me to be.*
>
> *After much consideration, I have decided to completely disregard your opinion but to incorporate the loving conclusions I drew about myself from contemplating them.*
>
> *Thanks again! Love, Susan*

*Thank you*

When you have cleared the stagnant air, add on a few hearty thank you's for all the goodness in life (I am grateful for my family! I am grateful for my home!) Use the space below and the facing page. Go!

Thank you for tackling that tough exercise. It is difficult to have an **attitude of gratitude** toward things that have hurt you. A friend of mine is an excellent example of how you can take something that devastates you and turn it into something that builds you up.

Theresa Byrne, a 4th degree black belt, entrepreneur, author and motivational speaker was in a hit and run accident in the summer of 2014. After a reckless driver caused her to careen off the road and into a brick wall, her car was totaled, but she walked away with only a few scratches and bruises. Or, so she thought. She was back at work the next day, still reeling from what happened.

As a few weeks passed, Theresa began to notice that she wasn't thinking as clearly as she did before and simple, every day tasks were becoming overwhelming. A month after the accident, she went to the ER for a migraine and learned she had suffered a serious brain injury in the accident. Her brain was severely damaged, which forced her to take a leave of absence from her career and, ultimately, her life.

For months, she had to remain mostly in the dark, alone at home, with no stimulation in order for her brain

to rest and heal. She had limited contact with friends and family. After a while, she began cognitive therapy to help her progress. As of January 2016, Theresa is still in therapy and learning how to live with her new brain, which functions differently than before the accident.

Here is what Theresa has to say about her injury:

> "There's a saying from Einstein, 'you can view your world as if everything is a miracle or nothing is a miracle.' I have chosen to look at the world as if it was full of miracles. In every single day everything that happens ... I look for the good in everything.
>
> So, when I was in a hit-and-run car accident the first thing I thought was not "oh what a miracle this is!"
>
> But, instead of looking at it as if it were some terrible thing, I used some core questioning techniques:
>
> 'Okay what is this trying to show me? How is this helping me grow? What can I use in this to help others? What's the gift in this?' I thought, 'what good could possibly come from this?'
>
> When I saw that five of the six lobes of my brain had been severely damaged, my pain levels were constant and that my cognition and communication were heavily changed, I was really challenged.
>
> Would I be one of those people always trying or attempting to see the positive or would I really do it?
>
> Those with traumatic brain injuries are more likely to (commit) suicide or become substance addicted because it changes the very core of who you are. Who you were. You stop producing mel-

*atonin (sleep), dopamine and serotonin (pleasure happiness neurotransmitters). So, I had to create new ways to cope with that.*

*I chose, instead, to see what I could be grateful for and to ask that question every day. And, write down my answers.*

*Every day I'm given answers to those questions, I look at this as an adventure.*

*Through the process, I found new ways my brain needed to work and new strategies to achieve things. The gift to step outside of me into a whole other new me (version 2.0). Literally.*

*I will never ever be that Theresa again so I'm grateful to be a version I have some choice in... allowing a new miracle that's me to unfold. To share her story and maybe it'll help someone else. To be at* CAUSE *in my own matter!!!!"*

Theresa's story is valuable because it shows us how even in the darkest moments, when we are sure we have been buried in shit not of our making, that in fact, we have been planted in the fertilizer for our soul.

The nightmare that Theresa was experiencing has now become part of a dream she has always dreamed of: helping others realize their own power in times of chaos. Her dream of power coaching through webinars and classes is coming to fruition. She has even been invited to do a TED talk on her experience! All things she had originally desired before her accident.

These new accomplishments are because she said YES to not being afraid of living her life with passion and movement, even when her world had crashed down around her.

In forming our game plan, movement is key to creating an atmosphere of change.

No one wants to stay stagnant in their lives; it is up to us create new opportunities and say YES to ones that come our way so we continue to grow. Gratitude enables us to see the best in the worst and helps us to continue to move forward.

The art of gratitude and movement is one that we will need when we encounter disappointment, which on this journey is inevitable.

CHAPTER 7:

# Divine Support

*"I believe in signs... what we need to learn is always there before us, we just have to look around us with respect & attention to discover where God is leading us and which step we should take. When we are on the right path, we follow the signs, and if we occasionally stumble, the Divine comes to our aid, preventing us from making mistakes."*
–Paulo Coelho, *The Zahir*

God and Goddess/the Universe/the Creator/Spirit will support you in this process. It's a fact. No matter what your belief system, divine energetics conspire on your behalf when you are in alignment with your true purpose.

The *Someday* you have chosen to focus on and create a game plan for is just a part of that purpose. It is similar to putting together a puzzle. When you try to force pieces together that don't fit, you are left with an incomplete picture and a deformed mess. Instead, when you take the time to find the pieces that fit together naturally, then you end up with a complete and smooth picture. The pieces naturally and seamlessly go together. It may take you a little longer and what you thought would be an hour puzzle has now taken you several days to complete. But it's done. And it's in perfect order.

When you are in the process of creating your *Someday*, the timing of it all can make you crazy. I am a product of the drive-through generation. I want it NOW! Sometimes, I even stamp my foot at the Universe, much like little Veruca Salt in *Charlie and the Chocolate Factory*.

"I want it NOW, Daddy!!!!," she screams.

I am sure the Universe is entertained by my fits, but in its eternally patient way, just pats me on the head and

says, "*When it's time, my love.*" That could be 5 minutes from now, tomorrow, next week, five years. Can I really wait THAT long?

I have learned that God knows my plan better than I do and is happy that I am FINALLY getting a clue about what I'm supposed to be doing, BUT the part I'm waiting for fits perfectly into my life next week, not today. I may not be ready for what I need to do until next year. So I wait. I sigh a little like that impetuous little girl, but I wait. And, then all the pieces fall perfectly in to place. And, then I smile and laugh at myself for thinking I know what is better for me than the guy with the plan.

How do I know?

I promised you earlier I would help you distinguish between Soul speak and Ego speak. One of the ways the Universe/Spirit connects with you is through your soul's yearnings. Your soul is tuned into your purpose and will share that information with you through your passions and dreams. Your heart's desires are clues to where you should be going and what you should be doing to stay on purpose. You always have support of the Divine; it's being able to shut your Ego up long enough to hear the Universe that can be a challenge.

**Soul speak will ALWAYS be encouraging and loving.**

Yes, it may sound like the voices in your head or even your own voice speaking, but you know it is truly your soul when you "hear" things like, "*Maybe this will work out*" or "*You are smart enough/good enough/talented enough.*"

When you think about the possibilities that are part of your passions, you might get a few happy butterflies in your stomach, a sensation very similar to riding a roller coaster. You know that feeling, when you are slowly ascending the first steep climb. Click. Click. Click. Up,

up, up the rails toward the peak. You are excited and slightly scared at the same time. It's exhilarating! Those butterflies in your stomach are in a frenzy as you reach the peak and then you plunge down and around and upside down, screaming and laughing at the same time. It's a good kind of nervous-happy you are moving forward and just a little bit of uncertainty in stepping out of your comfort zone.

There are some other ways you might be getting encouragement from the Universe that your soul may pick up on. You might hear your favorite song of encouragement often in your playlist shuffle, in the grocery store, in the car. You might be seeing billboards, bumper stickers, book passages, letters all affirming a thought or an idea you've been having. Maybe you keep seeing a specific sequence of numbers that has meaning to you.

The Universe speaks to us in many ways and our soul picks up on it. But, it is up to us to heed the call and act-it's time to move forward and follow those hints the Universe is dropping.

Now Ego speak is a different story. Remember what I told you before: Ego is a sneaky bastard. It knows your weaknesses and will use those to your advantage. It will tell you to say NO instead of YES. It will tell you that you CAN'T instead of CAN. It will tell you things like, "*You can't do that. You don't have the experience/training*" or "*No one will take you seriously.*"

Some other favorites are: "*Someone has already thought of that/done that.*"; "*If you quit your job, you will end up unemployed and living in your van down by the river.*"; "*Where are you going to get the money to do that? You should wait until you win the lottery.*"

**The Ego is NOT your cheerleader.**

Rather, it is a fear monger. It has its place when you

# Lies my ego told me

are younger and finding your place in the world, but as we start on our missions, it becomes a hindrance to us when listening for the wisdom of Spirit. You will not find its whisperings credibly backed up by signs or synchronicities. It may bring up old hurts and disappointments to make its case. Ego is depressing and sad. It is the shadow to the soul's light.

EXERCISE:
## Ego's Old Tricks

In this exercise, you will be taking a trip down memory lane. It will be brief, but helpful in your quest to identifying Ego's presence so that we may get rid of it.

In the space following or on the adjacent blank page, write down some of the putdowns you have told yourself in the past. This was Ego talking to you about how you can't do something.

For example, Ego used to tell me, "*You can't do that. You have no experience. You didn't go to school for that. You have no clue and you will make a fool of yourself.*"

Guess what? I CAN and DID do it. I learned what I needed to know and was a success. Now it's your turn. Write down those fearful comments from Ego. And remember: they are all lies.

Now that you have exposed Ego's tricks, you know what to listen for ... and disregard. The list you just made is a list of lies, Ego's way of keeping the status quo.

On the other hand, the soul is a constant cheerleader, and Spirit is always talking to you. It's your job to pay attention and follow your passions and what you love. I will take love over lies any day. Wouldn't you?

But, how do we deal with Ego when it rears its ugly head to instill fear?

CHAPTER 8:
# Dealing with Fear and Ego

*Only when we are no longer afraid do we begin to live.*
                                        –Dorothy Thompson

We've all heard the quote, "Feel the fear and do it anyway." The acronym FEAR stands for **F**alse **E**vidence **A**ppearing **R**eal. There are really only two states of being: Love and Fear. Anger, jealousy, sadness, etc. are all forms of fear-fear of not being loved, fear of not having enough, fear of being alone, fear of being rejected.
   **Your Ego lives in a state of fear.**
   Life is a roller coaster and your Ego doesn't like it. It loves to maintain the status quo — *Don't rock the boat! I'm afraid of falling in*! Ego cries.
   Let's take a close look at a common fear. A big *Someday* for many people is quitting their job. It may or may not be yours, but at some point everyone looks at their chosen profession to evaluate whether or not they are truly doing the something they were meant to do. For those who are yearning for a job change in order to become more aligned with their purpose, the Ego rears its ugly head and begins to fill their thoughts with doubts and fears. Here are a few:

> *If you quit your job, you won't be able to get another one.*
>
> *If you quit, you will end up homeless.*

> *If you quit, people will lose respect for you. You will be a loser.*

Remember, Ego is a tricky bastard. It will also say things like:

> *Don't quit now. Wait until the kids are grown/out of college.*
>
> *Just wait a few more years. By then you will have saved up enough money to retire.*
>
> *Is it really that bad? At least you have a job. Look at all the people who don't.*

All the above statements are based in Ego's fear. There isn't a one that is helpful or supportive of your mission. It's the Ego's job to maintain the status quo, no matter the cost. Even at the expense of your divine mission. Each statement is oozing with fear. Fear of lack, fear of abandonment. *If you quit, you will not be abundant. You will be unloved. People will shun you. Be grateful for what you have, stupid. Why do you want to ruin a good thing?* I'll tell you why you want to "ruin a good thing."

**Because you are dying inside.**

Each day the daily grind makes that rut you are stuck in a little deeper. Your emotional pond loses a little more oxygen and stagnates even more.

How do you stop this? You must remember that the Ego is a tool. It is there to help you survive, but not designed to help you thrive. Your soul is in charge of that one. Moving from Ego-based decisions to soul-based ones is not easy but it is rewarding and ultimately what will make EVERY. SINGLE. DAY. your *Someday*.

We must simply 'feel the fear and do it anyway.' Acknowledge your Ego's opinion on the matter, even thank it if you want, but do what your soul tells you to do. Give

# EXCUSES... EXCUSES

Ego a name, like Veruca or Sam. Pat it on the head and say, "There, there. *Everything will be all right. I've got this. You go play now.*"

Send it to a corner for a time out. Whatever technique works for you is the right one. I promise you that it will get easier. You will soon be an old pro at reigning in your Ego and following your heart.

**EXERCISE:**
**Letting Ego Speak**

We touched on this a bit ago when we wrote down our MI *Somedays* along with what we said no to and why. It's time to give Ego a chance to speak because little Veruca or Sam has been having a tantrum while we made them wait to talk.

Flip back to the exercise we did on "I can't." Rewrite those excuses below and on the facing page.

Those were from Ego. Also add your reasons for saying no to your MI's as well. It's all Ego. Don't be surprised if what you write is insulting, demeaning and/or rude. Your Ego might even use words that would make a sailor blush. Ego is afraid and will say anything to make you stop changing. It's okay. It's all lies anyway.

**EXERCISE:**
*Creating the Comeback*

Your Ego has had its say about your state of affairs. All lies and made up stories, but it can still get to you once in a while. Earlier, I mentioned giving your Ego a name. If you haven't done that yet, do it. Write it in your journal or in the space below. Next, we are going to create your own comeback to whatever Ego says.

Someone once told me that when dealing with difficult people who don't care what your story is or what you have to say, the easiest course of action is to stick to a one sentence answer that you repeat as often as necessary and ignore their rants.

For example, I had a co-worker once that would just go off the deep end about the smallest things. I would listen politely, then respond, *"Gee, that sounds like it upset you."* No discussion. No placating. Just a simple answer then I walked away. I knew I couldn't reason with them or even discuss a solution at that point. I just smiled, responded and left.

We are going to do something similar here with Ego. You are going to create a comeback that you will use when little Veruca starts ranting- something simple, detached and unemotional. A verbal pat on the head. Remember, your words are powerful. With this comeback, you set your intention of how you plan to proceed as well as make it clear to your Ego that you aren't going to put up with any of its shit.

For example: Veruca has told me that *I can't do that. I don't have the education or training to do it competently. Give up before people laugh at you.*
My comeback is: *"Thank you for your input. I've got this handled."*

# Dear Ego...

Don't do it! It's too dangerous. *"Thank you for your input. I've got this handled."*
You will never be successful at that. So many other people are already doing it. *"Thank you for your input. I've got this handled."*

With my comeback, I have shut her down politely and stated my intention. I have this handled. No matter what comes my way on this *Someday* journey, I've got it handled. Period. You may have to repeat this many times. That's normal. It will become less frequent as you continue making *Everyday* your *Someday*.

**EXERCISE:**
*Shutting down the Ego*
In the space below and on the facing page, write your comeback or comebacks next to the name of your Ego. Mine says: *"Veruca, Thank you for your input. I've got this handled."* What's yours?

Fear is Ego's tool to keep you from living your life full out. The false evidence appears real because of Ego's slick talk. Because Ego is you, it knows exactly what buttons to push to make you doubt yourself. Because you understand the how and the why now, it is easier to just say *"Thank you for your input. I've got this handled."* How

you choose to handle your journey also determines your success at living a life full of passion and purpose.

"This above all: to thine own self be true" is your goal now that you have your Ego in check.

CHAPTER 9:
# Integrity

*Achievement of your happiness is the only moral purpose of your life, and that happiness, not pain or mindless self-indulgence, is the proof of your moral integrity, since it is the proof and the result of your loyalty to the achievement of your values.*

–Ayn Rand

Merriam-Webster Dictionary defines integrity as *"the quality of being honest and fair: the state of being complete or whole."* One of the most important or *integral* parts of the *Someday* process is being in integrity with yourself. Both definitions fit well here. We must be honest with ourselves as to what we really need and want to move forward in our lives and missions as well as then incorporating (another wonderful word for this process) those wants and needs into our person to become whole in body, mind and spirit.

A fear that most people have as they go through this process is that they are going to go crazy with the newfound freedom around their lives. They are afraid that in the name of following their passions and divine paths, they will sell the family silver and run away to some tropical island touting that they are following their mission to save the world by lounging on a beach somewhere and supporting the local margarita economy.

That may be extreme, but it is a fear that may prevent you from taking action on your *Someday*. Being in integrity with your soul prevents this from ever happening. It fuels balance in your life and then the process becomes self-regulating. Let me explain.

I love to travel. I am happiest when I am exploring castles and ruins and learning about their history. I can get lost in a museum for hours, even days. One of my *Somedays* was traveling to France. My Ego told me for years that I couldn't because I had young children that needed their mama 24/7 and a husband that would starve to death if I weren't home.

What kind of mother was I to even think about leaving my family, even for a week? My soul knew this was vital to my well-being and my mission, and so finally I patted little Veruca Ego on the head and told her to take a time out from the fear chitchat. The family would be just fine. It wasn't easy leaving them for a week, but I did it, and it was life changing. It also was easier the next time I left because I knew they would be fine, and they knew it, too. It was a confidence builder for everyone.

My soul had been screaming at me for years that I needed to take that trip. It was privy to my divine mission and knew I had to go. But what I didn't do was use it as an excuse to shake up my entire life in ways that were not in my highest and best good. I didn't run away to Europe forever to visit all the fabulous historical places. I didn't sell the family silver or cash in the 401k to fund an extravagant trip. My family is important to me and travel is important to my mission. A natural balance was struck because I was in **integrity** with that plan. My family is part of my mission. Being a good mom and good partner to my husband is at its core. Travel and research in fabulous places are a part of what I need to do to accomplish what I am here for. When I am focused on that plan, the process becomes self-regulating.

**Making everyday your *Someday* will always be in alignment with your soul when you live in integrity.**

Beth and Tim Tiger are successful entrepreneurs who

MAKE EVERYDAY

also are founders of a philanthropy dedicated to the eradication of modern human slavery. Although already having a full life of family and work, they knew part of their life's mission was to be of service to others. Deciding to follow their hearts, they created Durga Tree International at their kitchen table, along with their niece. Living in integrity with themselves and each other helped lead the way in creating a balance in their life around their work and their new non-profit.

Durga Tree International grew by leaps and bounds in the first two years, heartily surpassing their expectations. New opportunities and relationships have appeared in their lives, always at just the right time and place. The Universe is working with them to make all facets of their life fulfilling. That is not to say that their endeavors are without challenges. Work is work. But, their mission is what keeps them on track and living their lives from their hearts in integrity.

**EXERCISE:**
*Putting your oxygen mask on first*
When you fly, one of the first safety rules the flight crew shares with you is *"in the event of an emergency, you need to put your oxygen mask on first before helping others, including children."* You are no good to anyone else in an emergency if you are not able to function. Oxygen helps you do that.

This is a rule that we need to apply to our lives, especially when it comes to *Somedays*. You are no good to your family, friends or your life's purpose if you aren't putting yourself first. By saying YES to opportunities that make *Everyday* your *Someday*, you are putting that oxygen mask on.

For example, you know you need to go back to school in order to change what you are doing so you are in align-

ment with your life's purpose. Your Ego and the sheeple Ego are telling you that that is irresponsible and will only cause hardship and pain in your life as well as your family's. Your heart knows you need to do this.

In order to be in **integrity** with yourself, you choose to begin taking classes online, completing coursework at night after your children are in bed. It's time consuming, and it's work. But, you are putting yourself first in order to move in the direction of your dreams. Your children aren't oblivious to the effort you are putting into this. It is inspiring for them to watch you pursing your passions and they begin to not only help you with the chores, but also work harder on their own passions. By taking care of your own needs, you inspire others to be brave and tackle one of their own *Somedays*. Your friend volunteers to help with your children when you need to go to the library. While there, your friend is inspired to find books on a dream they had long given up on. They now are moving toward making one of their *Somedays* a reality. It's a snowball effect!

While results may vary, the above scenario is not that far fetched. If you are not happy, healthy or fulfilled, your family and friends are being deprived of a great gift — the real you! As the saying goes, *"If Mama (or Papa) ain't happy, ain't nobody happy!"*

In the space below and on the facing page, use your MI *Someday* as the starting point for your oxygen mask scenario. Like in the example, follow the steps to how you begin pursuing your *Someday*.

In the example, the person begins night school. What are you choosing to do first? What are the collective Ego and your own telling you about following your heart? Then from there, write down how the important people in your life are affected by your choice. How do you inspire them? What are their own reactions?

# Me First!

You are not only fulfilling your dreams, but are giving others permission to fulfill theirs. Note: Ego may try to slip you up a bit here and fill your head with worst-case scenarios instead of ideas on how you are a role model for others. Now is a great time to break out that Ego comeback and send it to a time out.

Before we move on, I want to revisit the quote that began this chapter.

> *Achievement of your happiness is the only moral purpose of your life, and that happiness, not pain or mindless self-indulgence, is the proof of your moral integrity, since it is the proof and the result of your loyalty to the achievement of your values.*
> –Ayn Rand

Your happiness from pursing your passions and purpose is proof that you are on the right track. There is no place for mindless self-indulgence in this pursuit. That is the work of the Ego, which rejoices when you sell the family silver and run away to Europe or quit your job to sell meat out of the back of your van.

Making choices about your *Someday* in **integrity** with your heart is part of the foundation of making *Everyday* your *Someday*. And, when you are in alignment with your purpose and passions, that's when the magic begins to happen and the Universe conspires to help.

CHAPTER 10:

# The Domino Effect

*A positive attitude causes a chain reaction of positive thoughts, events and outcomes. It is a catalyst and it sparks extraordinary results.*

–Wade Boggs

First, we put together our plan like a perfect puzzle, each piece interlocking, matching up and creating a beautiful picture. Next, we watch as each *Someday* we commit to begins to cause a domino-like effect in our lives. The momentum of creation that honors our deepest selves causes more and more divine happenings in our lives. Our saying "YES!" to making *Everyday* our *Someday* brings forth magic and miracles in a waterfall-like fashion. One of the reasons this happens is because the first *Someday* lays the groundwork on which subsequent *Somedays* build and develop.

Since I have said YES to pursue my purpose and passions, I have been gifted with extraordinary magic and miracles. After I decide to say YES to going to Europe to pursue my passion, I was waitlisted on the tour I wanted to go on and received a note saying that although it was likely I wouldn't be able to join that particular tour, there would be one next year and I could be placed on the list for that one if I would like.

Less than 24 hours after being placed on the bottom of the waitlist, I received an email saying that for some reason, they (the tour operator) felt that I NEEDED to be on that trip and I was offered the place of someone who had just cancelled. Needless to say, I said, "YES! *Thank you!*" and from there, the dominos kept falling.

I met people on the trip that have become my closest friends. I visited places that have become the inspiration for the work I am doing now. A few of the friends I made have been invaluable to me in completing my books, providing not only encouragement, but also expertise that I need to be successful. Those are just a small sampling of the things that sprung from that very first YES! I continue to be grateful and amazed at the magic that keeps on showing up in my life around that one choice.

**EXERCISE:**
*Dreaming with Dominos*

Write down your chosen *Someday*. Imagine it has come to fruition. Give yourself permission to step into the energy and space of that *Someday*, which is now your Today and look at what comes next for you.

What is the next *Someday* that would build upon the original, now complete? You have the foundation; what do you do with it?

In your journal and in the space on the facing page, write down several possibilities and from there, several more. Design your own domino or waterfall effect below using just simple phrases and sentences.

For example: Travel to New York is the *Someday*, which you have made your today. You just got back from The Big Apple. It was fun and easy trip. Everyone at home survived. Now what? You have always been interested in revolutionary American history. In fact, you minored in history and started a book about it when you were in college, but your job distracted you from that passion. You decide to plan a trip to Boston and Philadelphia. Your family doesn't complain as much this time around when you leave because they know they will be able to get

through it and are even proud of themselves when they do. While on your trip, you meet a fellow history buff, who just happens to be an author. They help you restart your book and you finally publish it! Domino effect in action! Now go ahead and write about your domino effect!

Excellent! Now let's sit in that energy for a moment. How are you feeling now? Hopeful? Nervous? Whatever you feel, it's okay. It may be a good time to check in with your heart and/or a time to discipline the Ego.

How did your Ego react to your dream? If it reacted at all, hopefully you shut it down with your comeback.

**Ego has no place in the process of making *Everyday* your *Someday* or even just dreaming about it.**
As you will see in the next few chapters, dreaming is a useful tool we use in The Game Plan.

CHAPTER 11:
# The Game Plan 2

*There's a difference between standing up and telling people what you're planning to do and standing up and going and accomplishing something.*

–Paul Stanley

Did I hear you say, "*Weren't we already making our plan?*" Yes and no. You have done a lot of hard work so far with choosing a *Someday*, learning how to tame your Ego and such and even dreaming about the outcome, but now is the time to write down the actions you will take to make Today your *Someday*.

## Actions Speak Louder Than Words

How true this is in relation to creating your *Someday*. After choosing your *Someday*, the next step is to take action. That can be both exhilarating and frightening at the same time. Ego is about to work you over. But, you are an expert now on how to handle it. Don't let it get the upper hand. You can power through using your comeback and reap the rewards.

## Physical Evidence

After declaring to the world your intention to live your passions, it's time to SHOW that you are serious. You are not only showing the world, you are proving to your Ego that you can and will do it.

Physical evidence of **movement** is hard for your Ego to dispute. You aren't just all talk. You are DOING. What you choose to do does not have to be big. The overall effect

is the same, as many small steps will get you to your final destination. For example, if your *Someday* is going back to school, your physical evidence might be as simple as going online and looking at different schools. It could be applying for or renewing your passport if you want to travel overseas. If those seem daunting, dial it back a notch. For school, perhaps you would talk to someone in your desired profession and for travel, you could read a book on your potential destination. The possibilities are endless. The important thing is to DO SOMETHING. Anything more than saying you will do it *Someday* is progress.

A friend of mine is an ultrarunner. Ultrarunning is any sporting event involving running and walking distances over 26.2 miles (a marathon). It usually involves rough, untamed terrain and extreme weather. If that's not the norm, then she is just extremely unlucky.

A few years ago, she was introduced to running, and at first, she could barely complete a half-mile. She wasn't an athlete, or so she told everyone, but she liked the sense of accomplishment she got from running even the shortest of distances without falling over dead. Slowly, her distances increased. But, she still wasn't convinced she could run a marathon or even a half marathon.

She began reading about half marathons and talking to people who had completed them. She bought a sports watch to help her keep track of her run times. She spent time online looking at different races in the area until she found one that peaked her interest. Then, she registered for it, keeping the faith that she would be ready to attempt it in a few months. She bought a few cute running outfits and running shoes. She made sure she looked the part of a marathon finisher, even when she was still only running 10 miles, not 26.2.

Finally, race day was here and she ran it decked out

in her finest running gear. She finished easily and had a better time than she ever thought possible. Fast forward to five years later. She is now running 100-mile races (in only two days) through weather extremes and elevation changes that even the most seasoned hiker would be afraid of.

She didn't just decide one day to run 100 miles. She needed to convince her Ego that it was okay to make that *Someday* of running an ultramarathon a reality. She started with physical baby steps, not only because physically she wasn't ready, but also because those smaller gestures of intent helped to make the transition into that *Someday* gentler. Her physical evidence was finishing a run without dying. It was buying a sports watch and running gear. It was spending time on the Internet reading about running or looking for races. It was having conversations with runners. Each one of those is unremarkable on its own (except maybe the running part), but together they add up to success.

**EXERCISE:**
*Physical Evidence*

Take a look at your chosen *Someday* word or phrase. Take a few moments to get into the energy of your *Someday*, imagining how it will feel when it becomes your Today. Now write down as many pieces of physical evidence that you can think of that will help you make it a reality. Don't judge the size of the item. Just write them down.

For example: Travel the World Physical Evidence — research the destination. Research plane fares, hotels. Get a passport. Buy some luggage. Pick up travel size toiletries. Buy a packable hat. Make hotel reservations. Search for local restaurants.

One of my favorites is booking hotel reservations that are either refundable or no obligation. This seemingly insignificant action removes that block that "you can't" go somewhere. Of course you can and you have reservations to prove it. It frees your mind to make more extravagant plans. Now GO!

Now re-read your list. Number them in the order you will do them in to show the world and your Ego that you mean business. Don't try to figure out how some of the trickier ones may come to pass. Remember that the Universe conspires to help you and once you get going, the domino effect will be in full force. Serendipity may very well be an every day occurrence. And, you will be closer to making *Everyday* your *Someday*.

Remember how my precious Veruca always wants it NOW? She's going to have to learn to wait when it comes to *Somedays*, at least to start. Don't be attached to the timing of how things unfold. I know I want to jump right from A to Z and skip the middle part, but most of the time, the middle part is where our growth and learning take place.

**Invest your energy into dreaming about your *Someday*.**

Leave the how and when up to the divine experts. That doesn't mean you stop action on your *Someday*, waiting for the Universe to show up with what you need. Keep moving forward with your physical evidence tasks, making it clear to the Ego that you mean business, and watch your *Someday* fall right into place. I like to think of it as **Active Faith**.

I have faith that the Universe is conspiring with my soul to bring about fabulous things for my passions and purpose. All the while, I am taking action toward that end. One of the most challenging, yet powerful, actions you can take is **public declaration**.

CHAPTER 12:
# The Elevator Speech

*It is not the question, what am I going to be when I grow up; you should ask the question, who am I going to be when I grow up.*

–Goldie Hawn

You are now ready to make the public declaration of your *Someday*. Who are you going to be when you grow up and into your purpose and passion? You have proven to yourself (and your Ego) that you are serious about your future. It's time to take the step of telling the world that you are stepping into your role as… you fill in the blank.

That's what the elevator speech is all about. You meet someone in an elevator. You have 30 seconds between stops to tell them who you are and what you are up to. How do you summarize your greatness in a few sentences?

This public declaration of your *Someday* as TODAY is important. It is usually the final nail in the coffin of doubt and sets your soul free to be who and what it really is. When I first started telling people I was a writer, I would often say it quickly or softly. My Ego hoped they didn't hear me, but my heart yearned to be acknowledged. My declaration was met with enthusiasm and excitement, which fueled my soul to keep moving forward and extinguished my Ego's hope that I would go back to mediocre and my old status quo.

The words you choose to share your journey with someone, especially a stranger, are important. For example,

instead of saying, "*I'm trying to go back to school to become a vet,*" you could say, "*I am in the process of becoming a vet. I will be enrolling in my first classes in the Fall.*"

Do you FEEL the difference? The first statement feels like you aren't quite sure what you want or if it is going to work out. It feels like if it doesn't work out, at least you tried and that's enough. It's not enough.

"Do or do not. There is no Try." Master Yoda was right on. You will either do it or not do it. The try is a cop out.

**Try is a way of absolving you any responsibility in the failure (or success) of something.**

I tried it and it didn't work. At least I tried, but the world was against me. I tried it and it worked. Lucky me! The Universe has smiled upon me. When you DO something, you are consciously putting your best effort into it. It is calculated and thought out usually. The intention behind your actions is much more committed and purposeful than "trying." You may fail in your first attempt of "Do." You can DO it again or DO something new. Instead of give it a try, give it a DO!

**EXERCISE:**
*The Elevator Speech*

Before you begin the exercise, go back into the same frame of mind you had when you were doing the physical evidence exercise. Be in that reality and languish in that manifesting energy.

Who are you when you are in there? Live in that reality for a few minutes, then write your elevator speech below and on the facing page. Pay special attention to the words you use, only choosing words that are powerful and encouraging. When you are finished, read it out loud to yourself and time it. You want it to be short, concise and powerful.

For example: In response to "*What do you do?*" Well, I am writer and speaker. I have written three non-fiction books, two for children and one for adults and am working on my first fiction piece. My children's books deal with teaching children about angels and chakras. My other book is about living your life with passion and purpose. I also facilitate workshops about those topics as well as working with your divine gifts. I have made it a priority to travel around the world to research sacred places and learn more about the history associated with those places, which I am incorporating into my writing and teaching. I have a full life and love it!

Now write yours!

Yep, you knew this part was coming. Now you are going to take your declaration on the road. Give it a test drive. Declare it first to your friends and family, those people who will be encouraging and supportive. We are stacking the deck here a little because we don't want to give the Ego any sort of leeway in this step. We want the Ego to hear the positive feedback and encouragement.

Once you try it out on friends and family, move into casual conversation with acquaintances and people you meet throughout your day. You will find that it gets easier each time you say it and you will start to live it as well.

You aren't done yet, though. You will now move into the part of making *Everyday* your *Someday* that will test your resolve and allow you to reap the rewards you have been yearning for.

You have to practice what you preach.

CHAPTER 13:

# Practice Makes Practice

*Good ideas are not adopted automatically. They must be driven into practice with courageous patience.*

—Hyman Rickover

You look great on paper. In fact, you look awesome. You sound great in an elevator. Not just great, fabulous! Now it's time to BE great anywhere, anytime. The elevator speech gave you confidence to think of yourself as a person living their purpose and passions. But, if you don't actively continue pursuing your dreams that are in alignment with your soul, then all this was for naught.

**It is easy to speak about what we want to do. It is harder to act on that because of Ego.**

Ego doesn't disappear once you begin the process of making *Everyday* your *Someday*. It becomes quieter. It plots, it schemes, it mopes. It waits for you to stumble, then bombards you with guilt and anger. Ego will always be with you, but you choose what to do with it and how you handle it. You will have setbacks. That's inevitable. They can either be learning experiences or roadblocks. The choice is yours. How you deal with them will make or break your journey to living your soul's mission.

## What If I Threw a Pity Party and No One Came

When we have setbacks, we have to allow ourselves a little time to lament our circumstances. Some people may

not agree with me on this point. They might say that you just have to get over it and move on. Don't wallow in self-pity. I disagree. It's okay, even healthy, to throw a bit of a pity party for ourselves when we experience disappointment on the road to our *Someday*. This allows us time to regroup and evaluate what derailed our progress. Were there circumstances beyond our control or were they of our own making? Did Ego have a hand in it?

Once we know the cause, we can watch for it and avoid it next time. I advise you not to invite people to the pity party. In this case, the party needs to be short and to the point. Bringing people into your misery only prolongs the sadness and could also give Ego what it needs to plant a shred of doubt in your mind about your *Someday* plans. This is a party for one. That's not to say that you can't share your experience or ask advice.

Choose the people you involve carefully, asking only those who have your best interests at heart and are supportive of your purpose. Do so when you are mentally and emotionally prepared to process their feedback in a healthy way. You don't want your Ego or the collective sheeple Ego influencing your decisions.

## Practice Makes *Practice*

Merriam-Webster defines practice as *"to do something again and again in order to become better at it*
*: to do (something) regularly or constantly as an ordinary part of your life."*

Both definitions are applicable here. Practicing your elevator speech, practicing being in the energy of your future, practicing quieting your Ego are all part of the *practice* of making Everyday your *Someday*. Once you get the hang of it, these tools will become ingrained in your thought process and will get easier and easier to do.

The Practice of making Everyday your *Someday* will become second nature after a while. New scenarios and challenges will arise as you tackle new *Somedays*. There is no easy path to your *Someday*. You have to make an effort, or put into practice, those tools you have learned in order to be successful in living your life with passion and purpose.

As a recap, here are the tools we went over to help make *Everyday* your *Someday*:

- Write away your day to become present to where you are and what you need in the moment.
- Name and classify your *Someday*.
- Thank the crap — Attitude of Gratitude.
- Identify where and how Ego is influencing you and deal with it immediately with your comeback.
- Put your own oxygen mask on first. This is about you!
- Dreaming with dominos. How will this *Someday* cause a domino effect in your life?
- Create Physical Evidence of your commitment.
- Develop an Elevator Speech around your *Someday*.
- Practice makes practice!

Also, remember to incorporate **active trust**. Trust that all is in order and actively move toward your goals. You have the tools; it's time to use them to make Today and *Everyday* your *Someday*.

**EXERCISE:**
*Committing to your Practice*

It's time to formulate what your every day practice of living Today as your *Someday* looks like. We all have routines around our day. At the beginning of the book, you looked at what routines you have in your life and if they aid you in becoming present to your life. When putting your thoughts into action, it is best to have a routine, or *practice*, that we do daily to further entrench us in the reality of the *Someday* for which we are striving. In the space below and on the facing page, write down the practice you will incorporate into your day.

For example: I spend at least 10-20 minutes of each day in *Someday* meditation before I begin work. I take the time to write away my worries and burdens to become present to my life. I take the time to review the *Someday* that I'm working on as well as the steps I am taking to make that *Someday* my Today. I perform some action of physical evidence toward my goal in harmony with the steps I have laid out and deal immediately with any Ego issues that arise. I spend time in the energies of my *Someday*, allowing myself to be excited by the possibilities. I practice my elevator speech and take all opportunities to share with others about my *Someday*. I say YES! to any opportunity that is in alignment with my true life's purpose and passions. I am grateful for all the support of the Universe as well as my family and friends.

It's your turn. Now GO!

Good! Now reread your practice that you just wrote and pay attention to your wording. Did you use the word *try*? Did you use the word *if*? Did you use the word *will*? We talked about *try* and *if* before. They have a non-committal sense to them that doesn't have a place in your Someday journey. The word *will* is better, but still your subconscious is not committing to the present. Will is about the future. Notice the example above is written in the present tense as if I am doing those actions right now. I am not thinking about doing them in the future, which *will* implies.

Yes, I do them each day and some days are in the future, but there is a subtle energy difference between using present tense and using *will*. Play with your word choices a bit. Test them out by saying them out loud like we did in the chapter on words. Ultimately, choose the words that feel the best to you. Then, rewrite your practice with the positive changes in word choice.

With practice, your *practice* will take the shape that is the best fit for your lifestyle. There may be some trial and error and that's okay. It is YOUR practice, not anyone else's. Take charge of it and make it your own. You are the one that has to live with it and the results that come from it. Don't be afraid to experiment with new techniques or concepts.

For example, while meditation is something I enjoy incorporating into my daily practice, it may not be for you, but you won't know unless you try. You may do your best thinking while on the elliptical. My legs ache just

thinking about that, but I am willing to try it. Feel free to evaluate your practice after a few weeks or months to see how it is working in your life. Change it up a bit if necessary to keep the momentum moving toward your purpose and passions. Again, it is your journey.

**You will know what's right for you.**

CHAPTER 14:

# Today Is Your Someday

**Roy Miller:** *What day is it today?*
**June Havens:** *It's "someday"!*
—from the movie *Knight and Day*, 2010

Who knew that a movie with Tom Cruise and Cameron Diaz could be so inspiring? The heroine, June Havens, is making her Today her *Someday*. I won't spoil it for you, but this movie, even with its kitschy plot and fun action sequences, has an important message. No one is guaranteed a tomorrow, which is why it is critical to your purpose and passions to make *Everyday* your *Someday*, starting with Today.

You've done some exercises on living in the energy of your *Someday*. Recall how you felt emotionally and even physically when you are imagining it. The way you are and how you feel is the true you, living from your heart. It is the best version of you, which comes about from living true to your purpose.

**You aren't the same person you were when you started on this journey.**

Your perspective on your life is different. Your relationship to yourself and your Ego has evolved. Your thoughts on what is right for you have changed. People in your life may treat you differently. Some are afraid of your changes; you have caused them to think about their own lives and the choices they have made. This may cause them to lash out at you, discourage you or even abandon you.

Do not give these possibilities any thought. The fear you feel around those possibilities are of your Ego's making. Do you really know that they will be angry with you or leave you? No, you don't. There is too much at stake here to put energy into worrying. You need that energy to continue living your passions and purpose. You will deal with each obstacle as it comes. Use your tools to stay focused on your desired outcome.

You deserve all the goodness that comes from making *Everyday* your *Someday*. You were born with a purpose. It is time to embrace that job wholeheartedly from your soul, not from Ego.

**Living *Everyday* as your *Someday* is your birthright.**

In her book *A Return to Love*, Marianne Williamson says,

> "Our deepest fear is not that we are inadequate. Our deepest fear is that we are powerful beyond measure. It is our light, not our darkness that most frightens us. We ask ourselves, 'Who am I to be brilliant, gorgeous, talented, fabulous?' Actually, who are you not to be? You are a child of God. Your playing small does not serve the world. There is nothing enlightened about shrinking so that other people won't feel insecure around you. We are all meant to shine, as children do. We were born to make manifest the glory of God that is within us. It's not just in some of us; it's in everyone. And as we let our own light shine, we unconsciously give other people permission to do the same. As we are liberated from our own fear, our presence automatically liberates others."

This quote truly sums up why we are striving to make *Everyday* our *Someday*. *"Your playing small does not serve the world... And as we let our own light shine, we unconsciously give other people permission to do the same."*

You are not serving the world by maintaining the status quo, by playing small. When you feel the fear (Ego) and do it anyway, you are becoming an example of what it means to listen bravely to your heart and live your life on purpose, not just going with the flow. When you do that, the people around you become braver and begin to search in their own lives for their purpose and passions.

**We all win each time someone chooses to live each day in the present and on purpose.**

Remember that Merriam-Webster's Dictionary defines *Someday* as *"at some future time."* We are always moving forward into the future. So, in reality, *Someday* could potentially be this moment.

Start making *Everyday* your *Someday* NOW.

# Conclusion

*The cat was black, not tortoise-shell, but the smell of the sea air was the same,* she mused to herself.

She was comfortably installed behind the counter of the quaint bookshop, staring out the open door toward the ocean. Every once in a while a car drove past, interrupting her view, but that was insignificant compared to the interruptions from her former cube-mate who felt the need to share the gory details of his grandmother's surgery or last night's dinner with her.

Her life had changed significantly since she decided to live according to her life's purpose and she followed her passions of books and beaches to this seaside town. As if by some sort of magic, she found a location on the boardwalk with an apartment upstairs the day she arrived.

The shop was in need of some work, but her determination to make her dreams come true spurred her forward and new neighbors arrived serendipitously at the moment she needed a few more hands to install bookcases. Excited by the rejuvenation of the property and the moxie of the new owner, the neighbors brought books to fill the empty shelves and refreshments to keep the energy going.

Exhausted, bruised and blistered, she would fall into

a deep sleep every night but always with a smile on her face. She was living out her dreams.
**She was making *Everyday* her *Someday*.**

With her tote brimming with tourist guides, a bottle of mineral water and a cozy wool wrap, she waited impatiently in line to board the airplane. It seemed as though the people in front of her were purposely moving at a sloth-like pace just to annoy her.

Finally settled into her seat, she pulled out her guidebook on Scotland and stuffed it into the seatback pocket in front of her. It was a long flight to Edinburgh and she was determined to make the most of each minute, reading up on the castles, churches and gardens she was looking forward to visiting.

She was surprised how easy it had been to leave her children with her husband for her week-long getaway.

*Yes, she would miss them,* she mused, but she knew now how important this trip was to her future. She couldn't be the mom or wife she wanted to be without first understanding who she was and what her passions were. This travel writing assignment was the first step in making her dreams come true. The money she would receive for the article was trivial compared to the amount of pride and self-confidence she had already derived from being chosen.

Just as she opened the travel guide, a woman's voice over the jet's intercom broke through the drone of the engines as the plane made their initial ascent.

"*Ladies and Gentlemen, good morning from the flight deck!*" The voice was confident and friendly.

"*This is your captain, Marcy Baker. First Officer Mike d'Angelo and I, along with the rest of our crew, welcome you*

to flight 1440, non-stop to Edinburgh. Our flight time will be nine hours and 23 min with a cruising altitude of ..."

The sound of the woman's voice became softer and seemed to weave itself into her twilight dream of castles and cobbled streets. She had her first good nap in a long time, uninterrupted by children or telephones. Her *Someday* was now.

She smiled as she released the button on the mic and placed it back into its cradle on the instrument panel.

*That will never get old,* she thought, settling comfortably into her pilot's seat in preparation for the long flight to Scotland. A wave of gratitude flowed over her as she thought of the journey she had made, both literally and figuratively, to get here.

Her sister's unwavering support, her son's love and hours of hard work had given her her dream. She knew she was born to fly; she just had to trust her heart and say YES to following it. All the nights she had spent reading pilot manuals and studying for exams had brought her to this moment — 38,000 feet over the Atlantic with a $150 million dollar plane under her command and 238 people relying on her expertise.

Those facts both exhilarated her and humbled her. All of her choices over the last 9 years had resulted in her dream being realized. So many times she could have said no. In fact, she did countless times at the beginning of this journey. But she chose to say YES more often than no, and it got easier to say it. She became more confident and more driven to succeed with each hurdle she overcame. The process gave her the confidence to not only become a pilot, but then continue to learn and work toward her goal of pilot with an international airline. How happy she was now, with *Everyday* being a day she used to only think of as *Someday.*

# Resources

Durga Tree International:
www.DurgaTreeInternational.org

Theresa Byrne:
www.TheresaByrne.com

# List of Exercises

Creating Your Journal . . . . . . . . . . . . . . . . . . . . . . . . . 25
Becoming Present — A Reminder to
   Write Away Your Day . . . . . . . . . . . . . . . . . . . . . . 35
Making your Someday List . . . . . . . . . . . . . . . . . . . . 43
What is YOUR role in the flock? . . . . . . . . . . . . . . . . . 65
NO . . . . . . . . . . . . . . . . . . . . . . . . . . . . . . . . . . . . . . . . 73
I CAN'T . . . . . . . . . . . . . . . . . . . . . . . . . . . . . . . . . . . 75
Classifying your Somedays . . . . . . . . . . . . . . . . . . . . . 81
I said, "No" when "YES" would have been
   so much better . . . . . . . . . . . . . . . . . . . . . . . . . . . 83
Say it like you mean it . . . . . . . . . . . . . . . . . . . . . . . . 89
Turning IFS into WHENS . . . . . . . . . . . . . . . . . . . . . . 93
The Chosen One . . . . . . . . . . . . . . . . . . . . . . . . . . . . 99
Attitude of Gratitude? Really? For this? . . . . . . . . . . . 109
Ego's Old Tricks . . . . . . . . . . . . . . . . . . . . . . . . . . . . 125
Letting Ego Speak . . . . . . . . . . . . . . . . . . . . . . . . . . 133
Creating the Comeback . . . . . . . . . . . . . . . . . . . . . . 135
Shutting down the Ego . . . . . . . . . . . . . . . . . . . . . . 137
Putting your oxygen mask on first . . . . . . . . . . . . . . . 145
Dreaming with Dominos . . . . . . . . . . . . . . . . . . . . . 153
Physical Evidence . . . . . . . . . . . . . . . . . . . . . . . . . . 161
The Elevator Speech . . . . . . . . . . . . . . . . . . . . . . . . 169
Committing to your Practice . . . . . . . . . . . . . . . . . . 181

# Write Your Day Away

.

# About the Author

Since she could hold a crayon, Susan Marek has been writing. At first, her stories were about dogs and bunnies. Then, it was a comic book about a superhero car followed by a short story about the age of pioneers.

As we all do, Susan "grew up" and her writing was comprised of literary essays and research papers. Although her interests evolved and expanded, she never lost her passion for words.

As a writer, speaker and angelic intuitive, Susan has been honored to assist many people from around the world in finding their own passions, rediscovering their divine connection and developing their unique sacred gifts.

Through her extensive knowledge of angels, energy and human-divine relationship, she wrote two books aimed at keeping the divine connection alive in children. The first, A Children's Guide to Chakras, was named a finalist in the About.com's annual Reader's Choice Award competition. Both her first book and her second, The Children's Guide to Angels, were a family labor of love. Although written by Susan, they were both illustrated by her three children.

Susan's third book, Make Everyday your Someday: The Guide to Living With Passion and Purpose, reflects her devotion to assisting people in living their best life.

Although her writing has expanded to include essays, blogs, magazine articles and works of fiction, she will still, every now and again, break out those crayons and wax poetic about her dogs.

More about Susan at www.susanmarek.com.

www.ingramcontent.com/pod-product-compliance
Lightning Source LLC
Chambersburg PA
CBHW070604300426
44113CB00010B/1401